WHEN MINUTES SEEMED LIKE HOURS

This is a story based on remembrances of military and Vietnam experiences. Some names and events have been altered out of respect for the families left behind whose loss is painful enough without the details.

WHEN MINUTES SEEMED LIKE HOURS

Vietnam turned boys into men and strangers into brothers

By Domenic Russo

Gotham Books

30 N Gould St.
Ste. 20820, Sheridan, WY 82801
https://gothambooksinc.com/

Phone: 1 (307) 464-7800

© 2024 *Domenic Russo.* All rights reserved.

No part of this book may be reproduced, stored in a retrieval system, or transmitted by any means without the written permission of the author.

Published by Gotham Books (September 10, 2024)

ISBN: 979-8-3303-7689-6 (P)
ISBN: 979-8-3303-7690-2 (E)

Because of the dynamic nature of the Internet, any web addresses or links contained in this book may have changed since publication and may no longer be valid.

The views expressed in this work are solely those of the author and do not necessarily reflect the views of the publisher, and the publisher hereby disclaims any responsibility for them.

Dedicated to my " Band of Brothers", the Screaming Eagles of the 101st Airborne

To Those who have served, and to those who continue to serve.

To the brothers who are with us still,

And to those who have gone, but will

Remain forever in our memory.

"Now the trumpet summons us again… a call to bear the burden of a long twilight struggle, year in and year out, 'rejoicing in hope, patient in tribulations,' — a struggle against the common enemies of man: tyranny, poverty, disease, and war itself…

"And so, my fellow Americans: ask not what your country can do for you — ask what you can do for your country. My fellow citizens of the world: ask not what America can do for you, but what together we can do for the freedom man."

— Excerpted from
John Fitzgerald Kennedy's
Inaugural Address

TABLE OF CONTENTS

CHAPTER 1	1
CHAPTER 2	7
CHAPTER 3	21
CHAPTER 4	26
CHAPTER 5	29
CHAPTER 6	34
CHAPTER 7	36
CHAPTER 8	38
CHAPTER 9	46
CHAPTER 10	54
CHAPTER 11	57
CHAPTER 12	66
CHAPTER 13	77
CHAPTER 14	85
CHAPTER 15	88
CHAPTER 16	92
CHAPTER 17	97
CHAPTER 18	102
CHAPTER 19	106
CHAPTER 20	112
EPILOG	115

CHAPTER 1

It was mid July 1999, and the weather was hot and humid as it would be that time of year. I was packing my suitcase for a trip back in time having decided to attend a reunion with men I fought with in the Vietnam War. We were brothers; no, we were more than brothers. We were members of the 101st Airborne Division, the Screaming Eagles.

The 101st Airborne Division gained fame during the Second World War becoming known as the Bastards of Bastone. They were the heroes who helped to save the world. More recently they were famous for their heroics in the Republic of Vietnam. That's where I served with the Division. Now, some Thirty-five years later I am returning to Fort Campbell, Kentucky, where my life started with the Screaming Eagles.

August 9, 1965, I had awakened to a gentle summer breeze blowing through the window. The scent of summer was in the air. I was excited because I was about to embark on a journey into the unknown. I was 19 and leaving home for the first time in my life. I was itching for adventure, and knew I wasn't going to find it on the local street corner. So I enlisted in the military for three years not really comprehending what three years in military time meant. But it didn't take me long to realize the magnitude of that decision. What started as a dream of adventurous exploits quickly turned to a nightmare. However, nothing is all bad. I met some great men and made a lifetime of memories in those three years.

My best friend, who just happened to also be my uncle, enlisted in the Air Force the month before me. I remember having long discussions about joining together, but I just couldn't go Air Force. I thought the Air Force would be too came for me, too easy going. Being young, naïve, and just a bit cocky, I decided I wanted to be part of an elite, tough combat group like the Special Forces. So, my friend and I went our separate ways.

When a young man joins the military instead of being drafted, he usually does so for a particular reason. My friend joined the military to leave an unhappy relationship with his father, or as we called him, "the old man". His father came from Italy when he was 16 years old with nothing but the clothes on his back. You always hear or read about immigrant stories like that, but he lived that story. He may not have had material things, but he had enough backbone to start his own business. He supported himself, and later a wife and ten kids with the business he built from nothing. Looking back I must admit that he was a special person, but times were different in the

60's and his views on life were too old-fashioned for his son. So his son decided to strike out on his own thinking the Air Force would give him the right start.

I was interested in something that would be a little more physical. I wanted to be a rough, tough combatant. I was full of self-assurance and pride. I had pride in myself, and I was proud to be an American. This was before the nation lost confidence in our government. I guess I never did feel like the others. 'The others' meaning the flag burners and dope lovers. I wasn't much of a pot smoker and I never put down my country. That is one very important lesson learned from my grandfather, the opportunities offered by this country were taken for granted by so many. Those opportunities came at a price, and it was my turn to pay.

My buddies from the street corner had a different view and criticized and humiliated anyone that disagreed with them. Teenagers could be cruel to each other, but they weren't any different than kids are today. I'm not exactly sure why I enlisted except that I was looking for something different because I felt I was different from most of my gang.

After taking a battery of tests for both the Air Force and Army, I decided to go Army Special Forces. In August 1965, I found myself in the Induction Center at the Boston Army Base. The main assembly room was full of other teenagers, some with their parents, some with their girlfriends, but mostly alone and waiting for the inevitable. I didn't realize that most of the inductees were drafted. I guess the war in Vietnam was about to explode, and the military was gearing up for a long Asian tour. I was still just a teenager, and Vietnam...well. It seemed like a million miles away. To be honest, I really didn't pay too much attention to the news when Vietnam was mentioned. Little did I know what an impact that strange place would have on my future. This 'adventure' was about to change my whole life.

All of my fellow inductees were ordered into a large hall that suffered from neglect. It was old, dusty and infused with a musty odor. The hall had two American flags in front with rows of chairs facing the flags. They were the only fixtures in the room that seemed to escape the effects of decay. There were several people in brown uniforms stationed around the room, and they gave the impression that they were guarding Fort Knox. Everyone was respectfully quiet. An Army Officer went to the front of the room and ordered everyone to stand and raise their right hand.

"Repeat after me"...

It was the swearing in ceremony. After repeating several sentences, the Officer said, "Welcome to the United States Army" and that was it.

We were now officially members of the U.S. Army and as such, belonged to Uncle Sam. We were shuffled to a bus waiting outside to take us to the airport...destination, Fort Dix, New Jersey.

Flying was a new experience for me. I was excited and eager to get underway. I noticed the odor of stale smoke coming from the old upholstery on the chairs. The aircraft was empty except for 20 or 30 of us. So we had a choice of seats.

The wings bounced as we taxied down the tarmac. The first thing I noticed about this plane was that it was an old four engine prop-type aircraft. We were on the runway for what seemed like miles. The engines were roaring as we tried to get airborne. Once up, it was quite a different sensation. I could hear the wind deflecting off of the aircraft body. I could smell the exhaust fumes from the engines, and feel the bouncing of the aircraft in the minor turbulence. After a few minutes something strange started happening. A wave of nausea came over me. Perspiration started to trickle down my face and as the trip continued so did this awful feeling.

"Shit!"

This was something I never planned on ..airsickness! I had joined the service to become a member of The Special Forces. Special Forces means parachutes..., which means airplanes. What did I get myself into?

We arrived at Fort Dix in the middle of the night. We were welcomed to the Army by a voice in the dark. We were instructed to pick up sheets and blankets while we were assigned to a barracks and a bunk. Before I knew it lights were out and the day was over.

The next morning arrived at 04:00 hours. I was never up that early in my life! The alarm clock was a person pounding a trash can with a club. He was shouting instructions to be outside in front of the barracks in twenty minutes. It was still very dark. I noticed how warm this August morning was and the strange aromas in the air. The scents and sounds that morning were definitely different to me. This was not home, and I was beginning to realize that it was going to be a long time before I went home again, or at least it would seem that way.

From speakers hung outside on poles came a strong disembodied military voice bellowing rules punctuated by insults.

"You boys that arrived last night are nothing in this man's Army. You do and say nothing until you are told to do or say something. You are not with your Mama anymore."

He continued to go down a list of do's and don'ts. But, all I wanted was breakfast... *'When do we eat'* was all I could think about at that moment.

During the next several days we were issued uniforms, vaccinations, haircuts, tests, and more tests. We were prodded, poked, checked and rechecked; one of many discomforts we endured was the vaccination. A pressure gun was used instead of a hypodermic needle. The pressure gun worked by injecting the vaccine through the pores of the skin. This efficient method allowed them to give the shots five times faster. However, the number of different vaccines being ingested at the same time usually made the recipient sick five times faster too, but it was efficient.

When all was completed, we were packed up and shipped to our basic training company. Basic training turns boys into men, so we were told. All we really knew for sure was that basic training camp was our home for the next couple of months.

The first day of basic training will forever be etched in my memory. As the bus pulled into the company location and stopped. I noticed a Drill Sergeant standing out on a concrete platform. He said nothing. He just stared. I knew then that this was not going to be a great day. No one in the bus moved. As a matter of fact I don't think anyone in the bus was breathing at this point. Oh, did I mention, he was carrying a whip! If he was trying to scare us, he was doing a great job. He stepped up the stairs and into the front of the bus and started yelling

"You are now the property of Uncle Sam. That means you belong to me."

Now, if you can imagine a bunch of recruits stuffed with bags and baggage on a bus in August with no air conditioning and this person screaming at you that your ass was his, what would you be thinking? And there were five more lucky busloads behind us.

"Listen up! When I tell you to move off this bus, you will gather your belongings and immediately move off this bus. You then line up along the white lines. DO-YOU-HEAR-ME?" The majority of the recruits yelled, "Yes!"

I could see that the heat was even getting to the Drill Sergeant, and by now we were all drenched with perspiration. The outside temperature had to be at least 90, and it wasn't quite 10:00 A.M. The Sergeant took off his 'Smokey-the-Bear' hat... not a good sign.

"I'll try this again. DO-YOU-HEAR-ME?" The answer was a little louder this time, but apparently not loud enough to please him.

"I don't fuck'n believe this" he said looking down at his hat.

"When I speak, you will answer, 'YES, SERGEANT'...you don't say yes, you don't say ya, you don't say ya SARGE, you bunch of shit heads, you do say "YES, SERGEANT!' DO-YOU-HEAR-ME?"

Again, we yelled back, "Yes, Sergeant".

After the busload had answered, he asked again, "DO-YOU-HEAR-ME?"

With another roar, the bus answered "YES, SERGEANT".

Finally he said, "Now get off this fuck'n bus and on that line NOW, you bunch of fuck-ups."

The temperature felt like it had climbed to about 120 degrees in that bus. We were happy, no very happy to get off that bus. As we lined up, the sergeant stood with his back to us. He gave his whip a couple of snaps.

He said, "You recruits are the slowest fuck'n bunch of pussy's I have ever ordered off my buses. What is your problem? Now get your belongings and get back on that bus and I mean now!"

As soon as we boarded, we were ordered off again having learned to move with lightning speed, if we knew what was good for us. However, it wasn't quite fast enough for him so we went through this drill at least three more times until he was satisfied. We were so completely soaked with perspiration, and a couple of the heavier guys got sick to their stomachs. One actually passed out. The one that passed out was simply walked over by the DI as he made his way to the head of the formation.

He yelled, "by the time I am done with you, this main malfunction laying on my walkway will be 75 lbs lighter and will walk all the way to China if I tell him to do so."

The Drill Sergeant walked up and down the line. He made sure that he stopped and stared into everyone's eyes. As he walked by me I said to myself, *'please don't stop here'*. . I was lucky. He stopped at the recruit next to me.

"Where are you from, boy?"

The recruit smiled and said, "I'm from Massachusetts, Sarge."

I shuddered when I heard him say "sarge". The Sergeant reached out and grabbed him by the Adam's apple between his thumb and forefinger of his right hand.

"I told you, you fuck'n piece of shit-for-brains that when you answer me, you answer 'YES, SERGEANT'! Do you understand me now?"

The recruit couldn't answer. He just choked from the hold.

The Sergeant, "You fuck'n pussy. Can't you answer me?' The Sergeant was screaming, "I want a fuck'n answer."

The recruit started to cry. It was about then that someone from the back of the formation started to laugh. The Sergeant let go of the recruit's throat and ran to the back of the line. He pushed a recruit out of ranks.

"Who the fuck was laughing back here?" He then ran up to one of the largest recruits.

"Was it you, you fuck'n piece of shit. What's your fuck'n problem? Do you think that this is going to be all fun and games-you piece of shit?"

The recruit had a little smile on his face.

"You dumb son-of-a-bitch. Wipe that smile off of your face, now!"

The DI swung out and gave him a real hard smack across his head. The recruit almost fell down, but then he became so enraged that he jumped up like he was going to punch the DI

The DI said, "Go ahead, I'd love for you to place a hand on me so I could kick the living shit out of you before I have you sent to the stockade."

Then the DI reached out and grabbed him by his Adam's apple and spun his head around towards a building directly behind him.

"Do you see that building over there? That's our prison, the stockade. If you dare to place a finger on me or any of my men, after we've finished with you ourselves, you'll be sent there. Do you understand me you sorry piece-of-shit?"

After he was released from the choke hold, the recruit yelled.

"Sir, Yes Sir."

Ten minutes later the DI was still screaming at him. When he finished with the back of the ranks, he returned to the front again.

He started to address us as a group.

"You morons looked like a bunch of girls getting off that bus. When I am done with you, you will have lost all that baby fat. You won't look like little boys anymore. You will be men or be dead. Don't think that this is going to be a fuck'n vacation. Because you shit heads are going to be Uncle Sam's prized possessions when I am done with you."

His speech continued for another twenty-five minutes while we stood out under that scorching sun. This was my introduction to military life. I couldn't believe I had to go through three more years of this shit.

CHAPTER 2

Basic training was a pain in the ass. However, there was one thing we really enjoyed doing, catching the Drill Sergeant sneaking women onto the base and into his room. He would go into the local bars in town and pick up a woman. He would sneak them into his room; play with them all night, and then sneak them back out in the morning.

Nightly there was a Fire Watch Guard on duty in the barracks. One of us recruits had to wear a helmet liner, take a flashlight and walk the barracks for two hours making sure that there were no fires, and that everyone was in their bunk. At the end of a two-hour shift, the Guard would pass the light along to the next guy on the list.

At 12:30 AM, Friday nights he'd start.

"Where the fuck is my Fire Guard?"

The Fire Guard would run down the bay and stand at attention.

"Yes, Sir."

Then he'd direct them.

"I want you to go to the other end of the bay, and look out of the window. DO NOT, I say again, DO NOT turn around until I tell you that you can continue your rounds. Do you understand?"

"Yes, Sergeant."

When the recruit would go to the front of the bay, the DI would sneak his girl into his room. When completed with his nightly fun, he would do the same, except in reverse. He managed to get away with this for quite some time, but I think they were getting wise to him. Several of the recruits were talking a little too loudly near other unit DI's. So, it was just a matter of time before he was caught.

Basic was not exactly a vacation. We sloshed through mud; marched through rain; and fried in the sun. We learned how to kill a person with everything imaginable, a gun, knife, rifle and even our bare hands. We were taught military protocol and how to be self-sufficient soldiers by thoroughly learning the basics. I suppose that's how they came up the catchy title of Basic Training.

My first month in the military reinforced what I realized earlier, that it was going to be a long three years. Every week I could feel myself becoming stronger and more physically fit. When we first arrived we were given a PT test. The test consisted of running one mile, climbing a rope, doing chin-ups, sit-ups and many more exercises I never did before. All were timed. We were weighed and measured so they could determine how much baby fat needed to be converted to muscle.

We were marching with and without weapons for the two months, and barrack and locker inspections were done both randomly and frequently to keep us on our toes. This constant harassment never seemed to end.

As we progressed through training, we were used as base support on weekends. Some of us were issued trucks and jeep licenses. This allowed us to be on call as night duty drivers. There were times when we drove a sick person to the hospital or picked up a quart of milk for the General's wife. Other times we'd drive troops to the firing range. The cargo didn't matter. It was all gofer work.

There were a few older guys assigned to our Basic Training Company. They had previously served; were discharged, and then later decided to re-enlist. Since they had been out of the military for so many years, they had to go through Basic Training all over again. After they successfully completed Basic, they were given back part of their rank before being sent on an assignment. We all believed that they returned to the military because they couldn't make it out in the real world. A couple of these re-enlistees were real pains in the butt.

During evening maneuvers we had to crawl under barbed wire while live machine guns fired overhead accompanied by the explosion of intermittent simulated bombs going off all around us. One of the "old timers" got his jacket caught in the barbed wire causing the line of men behind him to come to a halt.

"What the fuck are you doing in my combat field? Every one of you are dead, do you understand me? They're dead because of you, you old decrepit piece-of-shit. I don't care if your jacket is stuck, take it off and leave it. Do you understand you sorry excuse for a human being. Now Mister, move it. GO, NOW, before I come over there and cut that jacket off of you."

As the man fought to take off his jacket, with no success, another recruit slid over to him to help him get untangled. The older man started to move.

The DI, "You stupid son-of-a-bitch, you just got your ass killed and probably half of your company along with you, just because you stopped to help him. You can't get killed without permission. Do you hear me, shit-for-brains? You belong to Uncle Sam. You have no right getting killed. Do you hear me?"

Needless to say, it was a long night, and the next day we had to qualify on the firing range.

Qualifications, everyone had to qualify with the weapon issued. Our weapons happened to be the M-14. We all knew that the new rifles being issued to active units were the M-16, and we would never again see the M-14, but we still had to qualify with it.

The M-14 was made of wood, it was heavy and it jammed more often than not. Now the M-16 was made of new lightweight plastic material and had very different and much easier to use chamber and sites.

When we arrived at the firing range it started to lightly rain. 30 Minutes into receiving our qualification instructions, we were hit with a downpour. The DI s couldn't stop because they would have to wait several days to reserve the range again, and that would place them behind schedule.

As the rain fell, the more problems we had with the weapons. The wood expanded and cracked. The chambers jammed causing many of the recruits to lose shots, and as a result caused loss of qualification. It made the DI's look bad. I was one of the lucky ones, I qualified then I passed my rifle over to another who had a damaged weapon.

One of the wonderful exercises that our DI had us do was what he called "kissing the dirt". He would have us line up in open rank formation and order us to hit the dirt. In some cases, it would be hitting the mud. We were not allowed to use our arms or hands to soften the blow to the ground. It was our chest and back that did all of the kissing. At the end of the exercise, we were completely covered in mud or dirt. I overheard another DI, one with a higher rank, tell him to lay off of the recruits. Our DI told him to mind his own business because this was his training company.

The men that I met at Basic were from all areas of the country. Some were drafted and some were volunteers. Whatever the method of entry we all found ourselves in that same place, that other world. The world that nobody, except veterans would know about. It was almost like being in jail (although I never did a stint in jail) except, we were not allowed to do anything at all, without permission.

The time in Basic Training went by so fast that I barely got to know more than a couple of the men. At the end of Basic my Mom and Dad drove down to New Jersey to attend the graduation. The 'ceremony' was not very formal. We merely stood in formation and were congratulated by the Base Commander, and then were issued our assignments for the next phase of our training which was Advanced Individual Training.

Advanced Individual Training prepared us for our individual military specialty. Some men went on to advanced infantry, auto or aircraft mechanic specialties. Whatever the 'choice', it would be our job while we worked for Uncle Sam. Most of the men who enlisted usually got to pick the job they wanted or where they would be stationed. By contrast, most of the draftees were not given a choice of either career or base location. They simply received orders.

My choice, as stupid as it may seem, was to go to jump school via Special Forces training. I expected to get assigned to an A team. It all looked so glamorous in the magazines and movies. I was sold.

Prior to leaving Basic Training our DI got a little too friendly with his hands, and banged up a couple of the recruits real bad. He wasn't a real big man, but his rank and demeanor allowed him to intimidate the men. Before we graduated, we were beginning to feel our oats. A few of the men decided that they weren't going to allow the DI to injure any more of the men.

His quarters were at the rear of the barracks. The barracks were wooden and had long bays with bunks lining both sides. One night several of the recruits stood on both sides of the door to his room. The lights were turned off at the fuse box. I could hear someone pound on his door. The DI came out.

"Who the fuck is pounding on my fuck'n door? The son-of-a-bitch that dares to be out of his bunk is a dead sorry son-of-a-bitch."

As he tried to continue his nonsense, he was hit in the head with a rifle butt. As he fell on the floor, several of the men kicked the living daylights out of him. They were, of course, wearing their boots. No, they didn't kill him, but he did land in the hospital. Some years later I bumped into an old Basic Training classmate of mine. He told me that he had met the Drill Sergeant in Germany. He gave up being a Drill Sergeant after he was almost beaten to death. He felt lucky that he wasn't killed.

After congratulating each other, I thanked God Basic was over and packed my few belongings in the family car for the drive home. I was officially on leave for two weeks. It was fall now, and the drive home through the changing foliage was beautiful. On our way home we took a detour to New York to visit my cousin David.

My cousin David and my Aunt Josephine lived in Brooklyn. He was left deaf after contracting polio along with some other bad disease as a kid. They lived lot of fun living there because everyone in the neighborhood was Italian, and in a brownstone where I had spent a summer when I was 10 years old. I had a everyone who lived on the street watched out for each other.

I remember my Aunt used to slip a monkey wrench out to the kids when it was real hot. The kids used it to turn on the fire hydrant so they could play in the water and cool off. The Police and Fire Department would come by and shut the hydrant off.

"Hey you kids, who's giving you the wrench to open up this hydrant?"

All of the kids would just shrug their shoulders.

"The water was on when we came out."

It was really comical.

This trip home was my first since entering the Army, and I was really looking forward to being home and seeing my friends. As it turned out it was no big deal. My friends disappointed me. They weren't as thrilled to see me as I had anticipated. They hadn't changed a bit, but why would they? I was only away for a couple of months, but that was enough time to transport me to a whole new mental state. While they remained just a bunch of immature kids who would argue about absolutely nothing like which branch of the military is the toughest or who had the hardest basic training. I ran into two of them in a local bar several years ago. They were still acting like idiots. I guess I expected too much from them.

Their reception was pathetic. I realized that I had moved beyond them, and their opinions no longer mattered. I decided that I would be better off focusing my attention on something that would matter, my next assignment. For the next three years my focus would be on my military career.

The discipline I had acquired even after such a short time away, made me feel pretty good about myself. When I thought about the lives my civilian friends were leading, I would think that it was all so very carefree. They were so oblivious. They didn't even realize that others were putting their lives on the line to protect the relatively comfortable life they were enjoying. I wondered if that was what life should be about, taking it easy and not taking responsibility! There had to be more to life than just existing. What kind of life would you have if you never challenged yourself? I only had one life, and I wasn't about to waste it hanging around street corners. I intended to put a lot of living into each day.

My military experiences, both in and out of Vietnam, were an education in living; although sometimes I believe that the lessons were more about survival, but in either case it definitely was an education.

The training I received in Basic had already changed me, preparing me for what was to come. I was mentally alert and more physically fit than I had ever been. I was ready for the next step. When my two weeks leave finished, I was to rendezvous with two other soldiers who had completed Basic Training with me. However, during his leave, one of the men decided that the military wasn't for him. His girlfriend was a hippie, and had convinced him that the military was the wrong way of life. So, to please her, he went AWOL.

The second person explained to me by phone, that he was heading for Canada because he had his fill of the military. I couldn't understand how they could just walk away from their commitments. Years later President Carter granted them immunity and welcomed them back to the country. I remember thinking what a kick in the face that was to all Veterans. It was absolutely terrible.

It was October 1965 and I was heading to my next assignment. Much of the reason I signed up for this whole military experience was the potential for adventure. They had assigned me to a base in Oklahoma, and so I was anxious to get started.

I flew into Dallas Texas; checked the bus schedule to Oklahoma; and found that I had a four-hour wait. So I decided to take a cab into the city determined to buy one of those big Texas steaks I had heard so much about. I stopped at the first steak house I saw. Instead of a menu, the waiter brought over a tray full of raw steaks and asked which piece or cut I wanted. I'm Sicilian. What the hell did I know about steaks? Now if you asked me what kind of pasta I wanted, it would be no problem. But, I didn't want to look green so I just did a little 'eeny-meany' under my breath and picked one. The waiter complimented me on my choice, and he was off to the kitchen. I must say that steak was the best I've ever tasted.

A few hours later, I arrived in Lawton Oklahoma just around midnight. The bus traveled from Dallas Texas to Lawton direct. The scenery was unlike any I'd ever seen. The wide-open spaces had nothing on them except oil pumps and rigging. As we turned into the Lawton Bus Terminal, I found that the bus station had a phone wired directly to the transportation desk at the Base. At that time of night all was quiet and dark with the exception of a couple of street lights and a few blinking neon lights above the honkytonks. The town looked like a run-down cow town you'd expect to find in the old west. I had the feeling that I was keeping the bus station attendant awake, so I decided to take a cab to the Base instead of waiting the rest of the night for military transport.

The cab driver dropped me at Fort Sill in front of huge doors that were attached to what looked like an old airplane hanger. The wind was howling, and dirt was blowing in my eyes and hair. The doors were so large that they proved difficult to open. After several tries I managed to get inside and out of the blustery night. The guard on duty was fast asleep. I had to nudge him awake so I could be processed, and get some sleep myself. He wasn't too happy about it. I guess if the roles were reversed I wouldn't be too happy either. He had a very low rank, so I made the assumption that he was probably just a flunky waiting for his time in the military to end. I was told that the CO wanted to see me first thing in the morning, then I was taken to the Headquarters Training Company, issued sheets, pillows and a blanket. Then I tried to sleep for a couple of hours. This was the start of the second phase of my military life, and I was not impressed.

The next day when I reported to the Commanding Officer I had a surprise waiting for me. The CO was a Captain and he wanted to discuss the Special Forces career I had chosen.

"Russo, your orders for Special Forces training did not come through. You'll be attending Jump School after you leave here, but not the Special Forces training you signed on for. You'll probably be assigned to an Airborne Division, if you still want to go that route." He snickered when he said, "I guess you're here in no man's land for the next twelve weeks. That's it in a nutshell. Good luck."

I left his office pissed because I had enlisted specifically to go into the Special Forces, now what. Later, well into my tour, I realized how much that assignment's getting fucked-up actually benefited me. At that moment though I needed to find out why I wasn't allowed to go to SF training. Later someone mentioned to me that I was not old enough. They were told that the age limit was twenty-one. That was the excuse they came up with anyway. Fort Sill, Oklahoma is a training center for artillery. I wasn't happy!

The Fort in Oklahoma was in the middle of nowhere. The closest town was Lawton. Lawton was a sleazy lowlife town with plenty of bars, prostitutes and an assortment of scumbags trying to bilk every GI out of their money. I never could understand how the government could allow this type of town to be the setting for a military base. The first time I had an opportunity to go into town, I strolled in and out of a block of bars. I had a couple of beers with a few of the guys, but it wasn't too exciting. At one bar, as I was sipping my beer, I felt a tap on my shoulder. Je was a woman. She looked a few years older than me, and seemed a little under dressed for the cool night air.

"Hi, Hon. How about you and I going for a little 5 & 2?"

She was almost on top of me with her lips practically touching my ear. I was still a kid, and I had no idea what she was talking about so I asked her, "what's a 5 & 2?"

She replied, "$5.00 for me and $2.00 for the room, Hon."

I was a little embarrassed at first, but then I thought about it. My first proposition from a prostitute! I told her I didn't have $5.00. I really did, but if I was going to pay for something it wouldn't be for her.

I decided to take a walk over to the better side of town. There I found a great little, believe it or not, Italian restaurant in Oklahoma. It's funny what you remember after so many years, but I can still remember eating two orders of veal Parmesan with spaghetti, and enjoying every mouthful.

On the way back I wandered by the local pool parlor. There was a girl wearing a dress that had slits up both sides and a top that actually allowed her boobs to fall out when she bent over to make a shot. She was hustling the men at pool. I watched her clean out 4 or 5 guys over the course of a couple of hours, but to be perfectly honest I was more interested in her boob action. I didn't really care about the game. It was a pretty exciting night in this little nowhere town. I was seeing all kinds of things I had never seen before.

The Oklahoma landscape was very different from the Northeast where I grew up. The land was flat for miles and for the first time in my life I could understand why the Indians fought so hard to keep their land. Once during a lull on a training mission, I decided to go for a walk. I walked around a small hill to find something unexpected and very beautiful. It looked like a rock quarry filled with light colored rocks. There was no sound, no wind, nothing at all, not even the sound of a bird chirping. Total silence. I have never forgotten the serenity of that place. It was absolutely breathtaking especially considering that most of the land was flat and covered with oil wells. Before leaving I had the chance to meet a real Indian, a very unique experience for a city kid from New England.

Most of the men training at Fort Sill were concerned about going to Vietnam. Of course the men drafted into the Army didn't want to be in the military at all let alone go to Vietnam. Vietnam wasn't concerning me. I am not sure if I was too young and naive or just plain stupid to realize what going to war meant. I just thought if I go, I go, no big deal. I wasn't going to worry about it. As a matter of fact I thought it would be an exciting experience.

I had met a Sergeant that had the same last name as me. We started kidding people about me being his kid. We met once in town at a bar that he frequented. I guess he knew one of the waitresses' pretty well because he was giving her the business.

"Hey, Susan, come over here and meet my kid.

She said, "Get the hell out of here. He's not your kid."

The Sergeant said, "Dom, show her your ID card."

As I took out the card, she grabbed it out of my hand.

"I'll be damned! Well it's the same name, but that doesn't mean anything."

We had a good laugh. The Sergeant was in charge of communications. I had a much better time going with him than playing artillery man. He took life kind of easy, and my time with him made the 12 weeks almost enjoyable.

Again I went home on leave, and again the time passed too soon. This time I was home for Christmas. My new orders informed me I was to report to Fort Benning, Georgia on January 2, 1966 for parachute training. When I was home on leave my old crowd didn't interest me much, so I decided to forget about them. Instead I relaxed and prepared myself for my next assignment. I was told I was about to go through some sort of HELL, and I should mentally prepare myself.

They were right. Jump School was Hell. This training made boot camp seem like the proverbial walk-in-the-park. A Marine Sergeant told me, when he was quitting Jump School, that it was the hardest training he had ever been through. He quit because he had had enough! I was very surprised by his attitude. I thought the Marines were all gung ho, but apparently not all of them.

The US Army jump school trained all branches of the military Army, Navy, Marines, Coast Guard and Air force.

A typical day in Jump School meant lots of running, not because it was the only means of transportation, but because it was one way they could force us to work our leg muscles all day long. No one was allowed to walk anywhere. The early morning would start with a five-mile run and a breakfast that had to be consumed within fifteen minutes. The quality and quantity of the food was the only good thing during training. The amount of energy needed to get through a day dictated large portions of high energy foods at each meal. That is probably why it tasted so good.

After breakfast we would have two backbreaking hours of physical training. The instructors monitored the performance very closely. If the training performance was found to be below standard or performed incorrectly, the instructor would issue a demerit. If a jump trainee received three demerits in one week, the individual would have to repeat that week all over again. One week in Jump School was like spending a month in Hell. Nobody wanted to do the time over again. I had never been to Hell, but Jump School had to be a close second.

Training restrictions required that we refrain from eating candy, drinking soft drinks or beer, or leaving the barracks after 10:00 PM. But, worst of all, no ladies! That made the training really tough.

A particular training Sergeant and a Marine Private somehow found themselves in a private war. The Marine bragged to the Sergeant that he could not be broken.

"You can scream at me; make me do pushups all day long; and run my ass off, but you'll never get me to quit."

So, the Sergeant took the challenge, and didn't miss an opportunity to ride him. They went on like that for several days. Finally, during one of their battles, a Marine Lieutenant, who was also in jump training, broke ranks and asked the Sergeant if he enjoyed picking on Marines. The LT. was tall, slender and hard as a rock.

"You like picking on Marines, Sergeant? How would you like to pick on me instead? Let me see you try that shit on me."

The Sergeant told the LT. that he wasn't picking on the Private, but that the Private had challenged him to see if he could be broken, and all he was doing was obliging.

"Well, Sergeant, would you like to try me on for size?"

The Sergeant replied, "No, Sir".

The Lt. returned to ranks and the challenges stopped.

I also remember running so much during training that I started experiencing shin splints. I don't exactly know what shin splints are, but I can tell you they hurt like hell. The pain was massive. Everyone had them, but no one complained. They just continued to push themselves both physically and mentally. I was in excellent condition, but I would still be in pain at the end of each day.

There was no end to the ways they could cause you pain, and pushups were one of their favorite ways of calling you stupid. If you did something stupid or just didn't pay attention during training, an order for pushups was issued immediately. It was retaliation probably for all the times they had to do them. One day I counted how many pushups I had to perform. I counted being yelled at and instructed to drop and give him 10 pushups 8 times in one day. By the time I had to make a parachute jump, I was solid muscle without one ounce of fat. Our bodies were so toned that we felt almost indestructible.

We ran without jackets or shirts in the January cold. Our hands would actually burn from the frost, but we would grit our teeth and bear the pain because we wanted to be Airborne. Every morning we would run. Every day the distance would increase until we reached 5 miles at a pace that would choke a horse. The physical exercise consisted of jumping jacks, deep knee bends, chin-ups with forearms alternating front and back, sit-ups and a few others that I can't remember.

We would learn how to make a parachute landing fall, by wearing a harness attached to a rope. We'd stand on a platform then jump off. A Sergeant would control the rope so we would fall forward, backward, sideways etc. It was a way of teaching us to make a proper parachute landing without getting hurt. We learned how to make an exit from an aircraft through a simulated aircraft with exit doors. We learned how to approach the door, turn and exit.

Inside the mockups were benches to resemble the inside of an aircraft. The training was consistent. Our lives depended on our learning and enacting with precision how to stand up and check our equipment; check the equipment of the person in front of us; and hooking up and locking to a static line. One of the most essential parts was understanding the need to hold that line so we wouldn't get tangled going through the door. Every bit of it was critical information.

As we progressed we were sent to towers that were 35 feet high, with pulleys attached. The towers simulated the aft portion of an aircraft. When we jumped off the tower, or out of the door, our performance was measured for its technical accuracy much the way a figure skater's is during a competition. Every element was important from start to finish including our knowledge of deploying our emergency chute, should the main parachute not open.

As we headed for the home stretch toward the end of air training, the 35 foot towers were replaced by 350-foot parachute towers. During this phase we were attached to an open parachute; raised to the top of the tower; and dropped. Since the parachute was already opened, it was just a smooth ride down to earth. On the way down, we were instructed by loud speaker to adjust the direction of our fall by pulling on the risers. By pulling on a combination of risers a parachutist could change the direction of fall. However, unlike civilian parachutes, we only had 4 risers to adjust. Maneuverability in a military parachute was very limited.

As the training ended, we were marched to the airfield to be assigned to our aircraft. This was the last week. During that week there was an outbreak of some kind of flu. One out of every three of us caught it. I happened to be the one. I was dead tired, and all I wanted to do was sleep. The fever was burning me up on the morning of our first jump, but sick or not, I was not going to miss it. I was not going to go back a week because of the flu. As luck would have it, the morning of our first jump, the winds were too high so the jump was delayed. The sun was out, and it felt good on my skin. I was able to sit back on the frost covered ground and soak up the heat in my face. It really felt good.

Eventually the weather changed and the waiting was over, and I found myself standing at the door of a C-119 aircraft at 1500 feet in the air. Flying in that plane was an experience all by itself. The C-119 was built and flown during WW2 and was nicknamed the "flying box car". It earned that name because of the shape of the body. It looked just like a box. These aircraft belonged to a local National Guard unit that was in need of air tactical practice. I guess we were the guinea pigs. The engines were very loud and the interior was not built for comfort. It required a long runway to get off the ground, and I could smell engine exhaust inside the plane. The noxious fumes were almost suffocating the men. It provided a wonderful incentive to make the jump. The whole experience was terrible. While trying to get airborne the aircraft would vibrate, shudder and bounce. But, once in the air, we were confident the "box" was going to stay aloft. Then we could settle down for the flight to the drop zone.

As we came close to the drop zone, the doors were opened and locked back. When that happened, the aircraft felt and looked like the rear was wide open as the earth passed below us. I was scared out of my wits. Although, most people would argue that I must not have had any 'wits' to start with if I was going to jump out of a perfectly good airplane. I guess you have to be a little crazy to do that. Now that the doors were opened, the wind was loud and blowing throughout the aircraft. Although no one spoke, their eyes said everything. They had the unmistakable look of fear in them.

The Jump Master started to go through his pre-jump ritual. The Jump Master is the soldier in charge of the jump operation inside the aircraft. He acts as the safety officer. He would yell orders and give hand signals at the same time for jump preparations. The commands would be given prior to the jump as the equipment's safety was checked. The Jump Master would walk up and down the aircraft visually checking each jumper. The harness and rigging are checked on the ground before boarding and after the parachute is installed on the jumper. Even though we each had prior safety checks, it was still his responsibility to be sure all was safe. Most of us were like a bunch of high school kids scared to death. I used to dream of making that first jump, but the reality is so very different.

Over the jump doors are three lights, red, yellow, and green. The red light came on when we were twenty minutes from the drop zone. The yellow light was the signal to get ready or stand in the door. It doesn't take long to fly over a drop zone. If we missed the drop zone, anything could happen especially if we were jumping in actual combat. At the yellow light I was placed in the door. I said a silent prayer because I was the first soldier, and we were the lead aircraft, Finally the light turned green. The Jump Master hit my butt and yelled, "Go!" I went because it was a reflex they started drilling into us from the first day of Jump School. So, when we were finally told to "go" for real, we went without hesitation.

When I left the aircraft, I was hit with a strong gust of wind. My legs flew up and my body twisted. I felt a little jerk and a tug. I had stopped falling. I looked up and saw that big beautiful apex. I thanked God as the sun shone through the parachute. It was a cool crisp Georgian February day, and it was absolutely perfect for my first jump. Although I felt relieved, I could also feel the adrenaline. I was pumped up. For me, the real fear was refusing to make the jump. I was concerned that I would freeze in the door; I had heard about such stories during training. Sure, we all talk a great game, but when the time comes, no one can tell how they will react. I checked my chute to make sure it had opened properly, and then settled into a nice peaceful decent back to earth. Logically, since the parachute was open, I knew I would be OK. However, it was still a little unnerving to be dangling 1000 feet or so in the air held only by a piece of webbing.

The sound of the aircraft engine was gone now and silence filled the air. It was broken only by the occasional voice of another jumper. The fall was so slow that I had to pick an object on the ground and watch it become larger to see how fast I was falling. It was very peaceful. This peacefulness came to an abrupt stop when a loudspeaker on the ground erupted.

"Check your chute, check your chute."

During the first five qualifying jumps the instructors on the ground gave commands to make sure that all the in-air safety procedures were being done. After an initial five jumps the paratrooper trainee is issued his Parachute Jump Wings during a brief ceremony at the drop zone. There were congratulations for doing a great job in a very difficult course, and the Parachute Jump Wings were pinned on our chest.

The general consensus was that we were all very happy to be leaving this training period behind us. It had been a difficult time. They were very tough on us, but I couldn't argue that they weren't fair. We were better off in many ways for having gone through it. We came away from this experience with discipline, a tool that we could use for the rest of our lives. There isn't a military parachutist living that could forget their Jump School experience.

After receiving my wings I was ordered to report to Fort Campbell in Kentucky, the home of the elite 101st Airborne Division, *The Screaming Eagles*. The 101st is the greatest fighting machine our country has. The Army needed men in the 101st and the 82nd so they disqualified several thousand men that were headed for Special Forces and rerouted them to the needed divisions. That was the real reason I was disqualified from Special Forces.

I had heard of the 101st Airborne Division. As a matter of fact, every soldier in the world knows of them. The Bastards of Bastone, the Devils in Baggy Pants were a couple of the nicknames given the 101st over the years. At Fort Campbell there is a museum that keeps records of the Division's exploits. Vietnam would be another chapter in the 101st's legendary history.

I arrived at Fort Campbell after a freak snowstorm. The whole Kentucky-Tennessee area came to a standstill because of the storm. They had received about eight inches of snow. Being from New England, 8 inches of snow is nothing. But I guess Kentucky doesn't have the equipment for that type of storm. The base had every soldier out helping control the snow, mostly by shoveling.

Prior to being placed into a unit, replacements were temporarily billeted until the paperwork had been processed assigning us to our prospective units, When there, we were issued jobs around the base. One day, I had to load coal into old potbellied stoves in classroom areas. I was amazed that in this day the military was still using such antiquated equipment. Another day 1 helped pick up food for some of the mess halls. I didn't mind; the work helped the days pass, and there was no pressure and nothing to bother me.

Finally, I was assigned to my permanent home, Headquarters Division Artillery. I thought this was a no-brainer considering I was sent to Artillery School. But, it wasn't long before I learned that Headquarters Div-Arty didn't have any Artillery so what the hell was I doing being assigned there. The unit was made up of Doctors, Chaplains, Lawyers, Medics, Aviation and Weather Groups, all professional types and support troops. I couldn't figure out why I was sent to that type of unit. I guess I was simply a replacement. My new job was "gofer". You know, anything anybody wanted, I'd go for it. I hated it.

I would chauffeur the Battery Commander around or I would drive the Chaplain into the field. I wanted action, adventure; this was a far cry from the Special Forces duty I had signed on for. The newly assigned members were summoned to the Battalion Commander's Office to be welcomed to Division Artillery. The Commander, Col. William Tallon met with us.

"The other men may ride you a little, but don't let them fool you. They're happy to see the help and replacements."

The Colonel was both physically fit and well spoken. He seemed to be well liked and respected by the men.

Being catholic and no place to go on Sunday, I decided to go to church for Mass. At the Mass I met Colonel Tallon and his daughter Mary Elizabeth. His daughter was a little younger than I was, but she seemed like she was preparing herself for something important. She was preparing for college, something that I had never thought about. After the introductions went around the Colonel spoke to me.

"Russo, it's good to see you in church, and not in town doing who knows what."

"Yes Sir, Colonel."

I was a little intimidated by his rank and stature. Naturally everyone wants to be noticed by the boss, and the priest and was no different. As the priest came around, he acknowledged me and spoke to the Colonel.

"Who might this young soldier be?"

The Colonel answered, "This is Private Russo. Private, this is Father MacDonald. You know Father, I think I'll assign him to you as your driver or aid. What would you think of that?"

I didn't think a priest, who was a mere Captain would refuse the boss. Of course he thought it was a great idea. It was a done deal, so the next day I was to report to Chaplain MacDonald. The Captain said he would call the BC to let him know. I guess it was official then.

We were in an area adjacent to the Chapel. It had offices, a small hall and kitchenette for coffee or whatever. As I was about to leave, the Chaplain called me back. He led me over to the Colonel.

"Colonel, I wonder if I can have your daughter Mary Elizabeth and the private stand in for two young people who are about to be married, but don't have anybody to stand in for them. Then later on tonight we all can have dinner together."

The Colonel turned and said, "Mary, would you mind doing something like that?"

Mary's mother jumped in, "certainly not. She wouldn't mind at all."

As a continuously horny young man, I began to check out Ms. Tallon. She was not bad at all. I was really going to enjoy this.

The ceremony was short and sweet, and the dinner went just as fast, and before I knew it Mary Elizabeth was saying goodnight as she was leaving from the Chaplain's car. I guess that was it for the night, uneventful.

Later I bumped into the groom in Vietnam. He was a medic attached to a MASH outfit. I had stopped in for a blood test to see if I had contacted some rare Vietnamese disease. I never saw or heard about him after that.

CHAPTER 3

The men were the most interesting part of my military experience. There was a real mix of different religions, nationalities, and personalities. We all had one thing in common though, basically, we were all boys in age and at heart. Unlike WWII when the average age was 24, our men were just boys with an average age of 19.

On the first day assigned to my living quarters at Div-arty, while I was unpacking, one of the men came over and introduced himself.

"Hi, I'm Guillardo, the Battery Clerk. If there's anything you need, just ask me. I know everybody and everything that goes on here."

After giving him the once over I said, "I guess you're the person I should become good friends with, eh."

He laughed and nodded his head. Guillardo was a short dark man of Mexican descent. Sometime later, he told me he was actually from New Mexico. He was quite a colorful character. I thought that he was awfully small to be a Paratrooper, but who was I to talk. I was tall and thin as a rail. Although, the military referred to it as being lean and mean, and who was I to argue with them? I took an immediate liking to Guillardo. I sensed he was someone I could trust, and that he had the potential to be a good friend.

After Guillardo left I finished my unpacking. My bed was towards the end of a bay. Metal lockers sectioned off the bunks. The middle of the room was open floor space. The men had a morning routine...shower, shave, then buff the floor. The buffing machine was passed from one guy to the next until the bay was completely done, all before reveille.

My first day with the unit happened to be Friday, and of course Friday night everywhere is the traditional night to let off steam. The army was no different. After unpacking my gear, I sat back and lit up a smoke. I noticed three guys at the other end of the squad bay. They were very loud talking about a bar that was located in one of the local towns. I thought I heard them call it *Shanty Town*. I pretended not to listen and not to be interested. Then out of the corner of my eye I could see one of the men heading towards me.

"Hey buddy, I heard there was a new guy coming in today."

He reached out his hand and said, "I'm called Zok."

I looked at him strangely. He continued.

"My real name is Harris Dubin, one of my shit head buddies nicknamed me Zok because they had a hard time remembering my real name. Who are you?"

"I'm Russo, Dom Russo."

"Hey, Russo, a couple of us guys are going for a few beers. Want to come along?"

It was a great idea. "Sounds great."

He motioned for me to come and meet the other guys. We walked over to the corner of the bay. Both men were tall and thin. I guess at our age and after the training we had been through, we couldn't help but be thin. Zok introduced me.

"This is Russo. He got in today."

He gestured toward a light haired person.

"This is Pete, short for Peterson. This other guy is Bill. We're waiting for Wishbone to pick us up. He went to get his car. His real name is Weber, Dane Weber."

They were dressed in civilian clothes. We were allowed to dress that way when off duty. We headed downstairs to meet Wishbone. I noticed an old shit box of a car coming into view. It had to be him. Wishbone was about my size, but big boned. On the right side of his face he was cultivating a monumental black eye. I'd never seen one so pronounced. No one offered an explanation for the eye, and I didn't ask. Little did I know that he received it in the bar where we were headed? It seemed that exercising with the locals in that bar was a weekly ritual.

The vehicle was an old Dodge. It had a cracked windshield, a lot of rust and smelled of a mixture of exhaust, mildew and beer. But it was a car, transportation, and that was all we cared about.

This was the first time I was off base with other Paratroopers. I knew nothing about the area, and if for some reason I was dropped off, I would have no idea where I was or how to get back to the Base. We passed a bunch of honky-tonk bars on a main highway. Across the highway were stores, restaurants, pawnshops and the like. It was a real circus out there, and another new adventure for me.

We drove for about forty minutes arriving at what looked like a roadhouse. The unpaved lot had cars parked in every direction making it look like their owners abandoned them. The cars were a collection of shit boxes and pickup trucks. Like most dives, there were drunks hanging around the building with some bimbo hanging on to them. The exterior of the bar had blinking neon lights with missing sections so you couldn't tell the name of the joint, but you could tell it was a bar. When we were close enough, I could make out the name, Shauny Town Bar on one side. A more appropriate name would have been Shanty Town Bar. That's what we called it. The dark shadowy areas of the building hid walls covered with obscene graffiti. The only area that was well lit was the main entrance, and every time a car drove through the lot, dust would fill the air and it mingled with the boisterous shouting and laughter of the patrons themselves coming and going.

We all walked into the bar together. It was your typical seedy place smelling of stale booze and cigarettes. Smoke and loud conversation filled this small dump along with a loud jukebox playing country western music. No one really noticed us entering, except the bartender. He flagged Pete and Zok over with his index finger. I could see him pointing that finger in their faces. I tried to position myself to hear what he was saying. I could barely hear him.

"I'm warning you two for the last time, don't start any trouble tonight. If you do, it will be the last time you'll be allowed in here. Do you understand?"

Pete said "hey, don't worry, we don't want any trouble. All we want is a few beers. By the way, we didn't start that last fight."

The bartender didn't want to hear it.

"I don't care who started that fight. Just remember what I said. You fight, you're out for good."

Pete motioned us to a table and hailed a waitress. Weber ordered a beer and as the waitress was taking the order, he reached over and rubbed her ass. Weber had good taste. She really didn't have a bad looking ass. She smiled at him.

"Soldier, how would you like your hand broken?"

He smiled back, "no thank you, Maim."

Everyone could tell we were military by our short haircuts and clean-cut look. We looked out of step with the rest of the 60's people.

Zok nudging Pete pointed to a table with two guys and two girls.

"Isn't that the girl you were with last week?"

Pete said, "Ya, and she wasn't a bad piece either. Zok, let's go over and say hello to the babes."

I couldn't believe it, they were just told by the bartender not to start any trouble, and here we were only a couple of minutes in the bar and already just a few minutes away from disaster. As they approached the table, one of the girls gave Zok a dirty look. She had long blonde hair and wore tight jeans and a red sweater that accentuated her assets. She stood up pushing back her chair and started yelling at Zok.

"Don't you start any fuck'n trouble tonight."

While she was standing there I got a good look at her. I was beginning to think she might be worth a fight after all. The other girl at the table wasn't bad either. Come to think of it any female looked good to us, anything with tits and a skirt would do. The second girl wore a mini skirt with a see through blouse and had long black hair. Zok was answering her accusation.

"What are you accusing me of doing?"

"Every week it's the same shit with you guys. You come here and start trouble. Well, you're not going to get away with it tonight, do you understand?"

As soon as she said that, one of the guys started to get up from the table. Peterson turned to the man and pushed his finger into his face.

"Sit back down if you know what is good for you."

"Fuck you" was hurled back at him.

At that moment Zok, from the other side of the table, punched the guy in the face sending him to the floor. I heard a voice behind me.

"There they go! Let's get out of here."

In an instant chairs were flying and bottles were being smashed. It was like being in a movie. It was unbelievable. I soon found myself looking up from the floor. I never did see what or who hit me. Zok grabbed my shirt, shook me a couple of times as he yelled.

"Let's get the hell out of here. Can you walk OK?"

I nodded and we ran out the door. Once outside I asked Zok if he knew where the others went.

"Hell, no" he said, "hey, they can take care of themselves."

As we made our way to the road it started to rain. I thought it was just perfect. How else would we end such a perfect night out with the guys.

Zok laughing asked, "Are you having a good time yet?"

About 20 minutes later, I noticed a car speeding towards us. I had hoped it wasn't the police or worse, some of those guys from the bar. The car screeched to a halt beside us. It was Pete and Wishbone in the front seat laughing their heads off. As my eyes began to focus a little better, I saw the two girls that had been in the bar. I couldn't believe it. I turned to Zok.

"How did they do that?"

We both started to laugh as we jumped into the car. They not only made it out of the bar with their heads, but they managed to take the girls with them.

Wishbone pulled the car out onto the road. Zok leaned over into the front seat to find out where we were headed. Pete, now halfway into a girl's blouse told Wishbone, "Let's go to the house for a few drinks."

Come to find out, Zok and Pete rented a house off base just for such an occasion.

All of a sudden Wishbone made a U-turn heading back toward the bar having realized that we were missing Bill. About five or ten minutes down the wet road we came upon a single person on the road hitch hiking. It was Bill.

"Let me in, I'm drenched".

Bill looked pretty ragged. His face was cut and bleeding heavily.

Zok, "what the fuck happened?"

"The two bastards grabbed me outside the bar and two more guys that were in a car joined in and did a number on me. Four fuck'n guys...Lets go back and see if we can find them." Pete had a better idea.

"Do you remember what their car looked like?"

Bill nodded, and back to the bar we went. As we approached the parking lot, Wishbone shut off the headlights.

Bill yelled, "There it is. That one on the right."

Wishbone quietly opened his door and went back to the trunk and removed a baseball bat. Pete reached in and pulled out a two-gallon can of gasoline.

Wishbone, "Hey I need that gas in case I run out."

Pete, "I'll buy you more, don't worry about it."

I knew they meant business.

Pete said, "no one fucks-up a Paratrooper and gets away with it."

Wishbone started smashing the windows with the bat until there were none left. Then he turned his attention to the lights.

While this was going on Pete was happily pouring the gasoline inside the car through the broken windows. The noise was beginning to attract a crowd.

Then Pete yelled, "stand back", as he lit a gas soaked rag throwing it into the back seat. The car became a blazing inferno lighting up the night. The crowd scattered in every direction. Everyone was racing to get away. I must admit, that I was a little nervous about the whole thing wondering what I had gotten myself into, but it didn't seem to bother the other guys at all. It looked like Friday nights with these guys would be a trip.

CHAPTER 4

Zok, Pete and Wishbone were a bit on the wild side. In contrast, Bill seemed too quiet and reserved for this crowd. They seemed an odd mix for friends. I found Bill to be very easy going, but at times as hard as the rest of us when he needed to be. I was told that he had enlisted in the Army from Grand Rapids, Michigan. It was said that he left a bad family situation. His stepfather was apparently very difficult to get along with and was especially hard on Bill's younger brother and sister. Bill had to protect his brother Bob by intervening when his stepfather picked on him. In return his younger brother, idolized him and grew up worshipping him. Later, when the unit went on maneuvers, I had the opportunity to find out just how great a guy Bill was.

Pete, Zok, Bill and I were placed on guard duty at the main entrance to the base camp out in the woods of Kentucky. Normally guards have two-hour tours of duty. Then the guard is relieved by another who is expected to be on for two hours and so on until it turns full circle or day breaks. For some strange reason, when we were on duty the chain of events stopped. We all fell asleep, and since no one was awake to relieve the one on duty, no one was guarding the main entrance. It was a good thing it was only maneuvers, because if this was a combat situation the negligent person or persons could be court marshaled. Naturally, we all started to argue about whose turn it was to be on and who was to get up.

"Zok it was your turn for guard, I woke you at least three times, now get up."

"Fuck you, Russo, I'm not getting up."

"Fuck me, no fuck you."

As the discussion continued, the Base Commander drove up in his jeep and stopped in front of us.

"What the fuck is wrong with you guys? All I keep doing is bailing you guys out of trouble. First Sergeant Pruitt said he was going to burn your asses if he caught you fucking around again."

Sergeant Pruitt, the first Sergeant, was the highest ranking enlisted man in the unit.

"Now cut the bullshit or I'll burn your asses myself."

Pete started to smile. That is all he had to do and the rest of us started laughing. Even Captain Goodbolt started to snicker.

"Oh shit!" Goodbolt said laughingly as he turned to his driver, Bob Evers.

"Let's get the fuck out of here. What a fuck'n group."

If the Commander had been anyone other than Goodbolt, we probably would have been put in the stockade.

Another time, again while we were on maneuvers, the same thing happened. The First Sergeant, untimely for us, decided to relieve himself during the night and noticed that no one was on guard. When the First Sergeant realized that no one was guarding the post, he started to yell.

"Who the fuck is on post here?"

We all heard him, but none of us dared to answer. Again, he screamed, "I SAID, WHO THE FUCK IS ON POST HERE?" After a few seconds of silence, Bill spoke up.

"I am, First Sergeant."

Pruitt said, "If you're on post what the fuck are you doing in your sleeping bag?"

As quickly as Bill could think he said, "I was cold. I was just trying to stay warm."

We all sighed with relief, thankful that Bill had the balls to take the blame. It could have been disastrous for him, and he knew it. His penalty could have been an article 15. An Article 15 is smaller than a court martial, but what it does is allow the Commander to present you with a fine, reduction in wages, or loss of rank, and maybe all three. After that night, we knew we could count on him. He saved our asses, and we were grateful.

Bill was such a great guy. I don't remember ever having a disagreement with him One weekend he decided to come with me to Nashville. Nashville was a little bit of a ride by motorcycle, and that was all the transportation we had in those days. The length of the ride didn't bother me because I made the trip often. I made the trip frequently because I was fooling around with a student nurse who was attending, of all things, an all-girl Catholic nursing school.

She had a girlfriend that would not let her out of her sight. She was kind of a Mother Superior type, so she became Bill's mission this trip. I knew she would succumb to that masculine charm of his. We had a little strategy session before picking them up.

"Look, Bill, whatever you do, keep her busy. I'm going to sneak this girl up to my room for a while. Why don't you take her for a walk or something, OK?"

Back then it was almost impossible to rent a room, and have a girl come up to visit. The front desk clerk at this hotel kept a watchful eye out. He had already warned me about sneaking people up to the room. Bill looked puzzled.

"I don't understand what you expect me to do with her."

"Bill, just keep her busy for a couple of hours. You have to come through for me with this….OK?"

Bill, "I guess so."

When I finally got her to the room, she let out a sigh of relief.

"Boy I never thought I would get away from her. Shall I go into the bathroom and freshen up?" I was amazed. She was reading my mind.

She continued, "I couldn't wait to get that hard body of yours up here. You poor boy. You've been cooped up on that base without any women all week. What can I do to make you comfortable? I think we're going to have some great fun tonight." She said as she pressed her wholesome body against me. She was correct in her assumption. We did have a great time that night. I later learned that Bill didn't do too badly himself. Her friend seemed to melt under his charm. He never mentioned that he had a way with women.

Al, short for Alberta, was a sweet 19-year-old farmer's daughter from Lebanon, Tennessee. She was a nice person, and we always had a great time together whenever I came to Nashville. However, her friends were dead set against her entertaining me.

Military personnel were not popular during the 60's. The 60's practiced free love, flower power and all that kind of bullshit, and fraternizing with the military was a no-no. Alberta didn't seem to mind though. She really seemed to enjoy having me around. She was fun, and we both had fun learning a lot about what our young bodies could do together. We enjoyed our exploring whenever we had the chance.

We had a good time whenever we were together, and for me that was enough. With Vietnam ahead of me, I was packing in all of the good times I could because it would be a long time before I would enjoy myself again.

CHAPTER 5

When the unit deployed to Vietnam, Bill and Pete became very close. Their two personalities complimented one another. Pete was the type of person that took advantage of everyone and everything he could. I can remember when he talked the Commander, Captain Goodbolt, into letting him be a lifeguard for the summer at a local pool. Not only did the Commander let Pete work as a lifeguard, but he also let Zok go with him. Pete had that effect on people; one day you would hate him, and the next day he would be your good friend.

In the states Zok and Pete were the team. They rented a house off post for parties. There was one lady in particular that became a live-in. She was hiding from her husband, and being such great guys, Zok and Pete allowed her to stay and even *consoled* her there nightly. I did have the opportunity to meet her once. She was a redhead and carried a very nice body. Of course she always wore clothes that accentuated the positive. That is when she bothered to wear clothes. She had what we called in those days a "Tough Hard Body". Those were the days of the sexual revolution, but you couldn't have proven it by the little bit of action I could scrounge up. I must have been very near sighted because I couldn't find any of those all night free sex parties that I'd read about. That's why I started hanging with Pete and Zok. I needed the action. The house had become known for having the wildest parties in the area.

During one of the parties the redhead's husband and four of his friends crashed through the door wheeling baseball bats. The shit hit the fan that night! By the time the night was over and the cops left, the house was virtually worthless. Doors were smashed and ripped off their frames, the walls had holes in them, and the windows were no longer there. The damage was total. The two of them knew they were in

Several days later the owner, an officer at Fort Campbell, saw the remnants of what used to be his house. He went to the Battery Commander, and demanded that the two of them be jailed. He also demanded that the house be reconstructed. He wanted his money on the spot, or he was going to have them arrested. Both Zok and Pete sat very quietly as the owner went on ranting and raving. They frowned when it was necessary and smiled when needed.

Captain Goodbolt talked the officer into allowing them to make monthly payments for the damages, with interest. He made the deal sound so good that the owner's greed got the best of him, especially when he heard interest along with the payment of lost rent. He accepted the terms.

Zok, Harris Dubin, was from Philadelphia. You could never tell what was on his mind. When he wasn't causing some commotion, he was very quiet and subdued. I never could quite figure out what he was doing in the military. He was a hippie in a uniform. I liked Zok, although I did think he was a little strange. His job in the States was armament. He was in charge of all the units' weapons. In Vietnam, he was assigned as a door gunner on one of our hueys. A Huey is a utility helicopter, the main workhorse of the Vietnam War. Zok did his job very well, and I admired him for it. For a hippie in uniform, he performed his duties admirably.

We were all a little lazy, but what teenager isn't? In the States we were in a state of constant combat readiness. That made our lives a bit more hectic than the usual teenager's. Every morning we were expected to participate in physical training along with the five-mile run. I hated it the first thing in the morning, and so did most of the other guys. One morning, as I dragged myself out to formation, I noticed that Zok wasn't there. *Where did that bastard go?* The next morning, I noticed that not only wasn't Zok there, but Pete was now missing. What kind of bullshit is this? The third day I noticed that Zok, Pete and now Bill were missing. All right, I thought, I've had enough of this! It was apparent that they had found a place to hide or an excuse not to be there. On the fourth day I decided not to let them out of my sight. The trail led me to the Armament Room. One knock and the door should be opened. I knocked on the door and no one answered. I knocked again and still nothing. The bastards were not going to answer. I was pissed, so the following morning I went to the room nice and early. This time when I knocked on the door.

Zok answered, "yo!"

I said, "Let me in."

Zok, "No. There will be too many of us missing. We're going to be up shits creek if they notice that all of us are missing PT."

Little did we realize that we were only hurting ourselves. The next time we went on maneuvers we felt like we were dying. We couldn't keep up. The missed PT sessions showed in our lack of stamina. We didn't have the energy we needed to both parachute into the area and participate in maneuvers all day. Although we were never caught, we pledged not to miss PT again.

One evening we had an early jump about 7:00 PM. It was still daylight as we adjusted our harness and attached all of the other paraphernalia we needed for a jump into a combat situation. It was very awkward to move about in our parachutes loaded with equipment, ammunition and food.

This night's jump was going to be an all-night maneuver. We were to jump into the drop zone under the cover of darkness. The drop included jeeps, trucks, artillery pieces and all of the other equipment to fuel an initial offensive attack. Once on the ground it was our responsibility to meet and check in at a predetermined location, store our parachutes and prepare for a long night's march.

Shortly after we entered the C-130 Aircraft, it started to rain. It was raining heavy enough for the pilot to decide to wait until the initial front came through before continuing. There were ten aircraft participating in this exercise. Six carried men, and four carried large equipment such as trucks, jeeps and artillery pieces.

As daylight began to fade, lights inside of the aircraft turned from white to red. This allowed our eyes to become accustomed to the outside darkness.....night vision. As usual we could smell the engine exhaust throughout the aircraft. It was a noxious smell, but then this wasn't a First Class flight...this was military flying.

Once the breaks were released, with a little taxiing and run up space, the aircraft felt like it would fly straight up. The C-130 was a powerful and versatile aircraft. We usually settled back into webbed harness seating with all of our equipment, and hoped that it would be a short flight. Trying to take a short nap was a challenge because the Air Force would practice their combat flight maneuvers en route to the drop zone. The nap, if we could get one, would also help us cope with airsickness? Flight maneuvers required what we called hedge hopping, flying up, down and around the trees, and was done to stay low and out of radar range. After an hour of hedge hopping, many of the troops were sick, and more than eager to get out of the aircraft.

As the aircraft began the approach to the drop zone, the pilot would begin an altitude climb. This is commonly known as a "pop up jump". When the aircraft hits the drop altitude, while climbing, the troops are released.

That was our sign to stand in the door waiting for the green light. The green light was the 'go' signal. The men would automatically approach and jump out of two doors, one right and one left simultaneously.

During the flight as the time grew nearer to the jump, the anxiety started to build turning into an adrenaline rush. When the light turned green, my heart would skip a beat. The door seemed to come closer to me than me to it, as the men in front of me passed through it. Suddenly there were no more men left in front of me. It was my turn to step through that opened door. What kind of insanity makes a man do this?

While you are going through it, everything seems to happen in slow motion. The wind slapped me in the face with its cold hands. I reached outside of the aircraft to find the outer skin for something rigid to help push myself out and off against. All at once I was off—out—and free, jumping into what seems, at least at that moment, like a dark abyss.

The blast of wind from the aircraft forced my legs up, swinging my body around twisting it sideways. I started my count, 1-1000, 2-1000, 3-1000, 4-1000, then felt the jerk of the chute. What a glorious feeling when it opens, not to mention, what a relief.

As paratroopers, we were always told that if we ever felt that we had mastered jumping, and were no longer afraid, then it was time to quit jumping. If we lost that fear, we would become careless and invite injury.

My chute opened, and as I floated down through the silent night I could see the other jumpers' faces illuminated by the moonlight. There was tension on their heroic faces, although no one probably thought of themselves as heroic at the time. The heroics would come later. These men were training for combat to protect our country at a time when some chose to burn our flag, ridicule our government, and hide from their duty. Some flew to Canada, while some of us flew to Vietnam fulfilling our duty as responsible citizens choosing to defend a way of life, and sometimes paying with their lives.

We all knew what was waiting for us once we hit the ground...water! With the heavy rains the day before, we knew that it was going to be soaking wet below. As I approached the ground, I could just about make out the tree line against the sky. The men's voices below me were growing louder, and I heard one of them above the others.

"Watch out for the water. Try to steer to your left."

Before there was time to react, three feet of iced cold water engulfed me soaking through to my skin. The only body part that stayed dry was my left arm. It just sucked! We had to be out there all night too. I couldn't believe it.

As I tried to find my way out of my wet, tangled parachute, I heard someone yell.

"Heads up men. Trucks being dropped."

I could just barely hear the aircraft let alone make out the equipment as it was being dropped from overhead. I had to get out of that chute and water fast.

It was so dark that barely more than a silhouette of the men could be seen loading equipment into one of the parachuted trucks. It was going to be a long night for walking to the rendezvous point. I was frozen to the bone after several hours of hard walking with water sloshing through my jump boots.

The sun finally looked like it might start to break through giving us some much needed heat. I needed that heat. Night maneuvers were meant to prepare us for battle. So, by their nature, they were not easy. Walking in complete darkness, trying to locate trails and contact points is a challenge. Add lack of sleep, less than ideal weather conditions, and hunger all while trying not to be detected by a practice enemy force. That was our mission. We were soldiers, and they were trying to teach us to not only defend ourselves and protect others, but survival skills that may just save our lives when we were no longer practicing, but confronting the real enemy.

As the sun started to give off some heat, we figured that we were very close to our rendezvous point. Since daylight was dawning, we had to be more aware of our surroundings, trying to spot the enemy before they spotted us. Ahead the point man gave a hand signal. Something was moving up ahead. We quietly took cover in the still wet vegetation. We could hear men talking accompanied by the sounds of equipment and vehicles we did not want to confront. We laid low trying to disappear in the wet grass and brush until they passed. When we felt it was safe we moved on through an opening in the path. We found our trucks parked and waiting for us. The night maneuvers were over, at least for today.

When we returned to the barracks, we had meals waiting for us. This was the first time we had a meal since the start of the maneuvers the night before. It may not seem like a long time, but when you're young and continuously moving all night, you can work up quite an appetite. After I had eaten, I slept for the rest of that day and all of that evening. We were in the best shape of our lives, but we were still exhausted after these all-nighters. What could we look forward to in Vietnam when our lives really did depend on what we learned here, and where there would be no comfortable beds to climb into after a long night. We had a lot to learn and not much time to do it.

CHAPTER 6

Wishbone was from Maryland. The only thing I knew about him was that he dropped out of high school. Like most of us at his age, he didn't know what he wanted to do with his life so he joined the military. Dane and I were friendly, but we never interacted one to one. We were always with the other people. I really thought that Dane would be a lifer. He seemed a natural for a military career.

I was the last one to join the group, Dom Russo, or known just as Russo. I guess I joined the military to prove something to myself and probably to my so called 'friends' back home. When I enlisted, I really had no idea what I wanted to do with my life. 1 really don't have a story. I was looking for a change and some sort of adventure, not unlike millions of other young men.

About now I was beginning to realize that my military career was not going to amount to much as long as I was an enlisted man. Don't get me wrong, the enlisted man is the backbone of the military, but I wanted more out of my military experience, especially when I had three years to serve. I wanted to be treated with respect, but for that to happen I had to move up in rank. "Rank has its privileges"...that was my incentive. I spent a lot of time thinking of ways to beat the system. I am sure many others tried, but I was determined to succeed. I had to succeed, because I couldn't stand the work I was doing or the living quarters given to enlisted men. So, I made it my mission to take advantage of any opportunity.

Our day started at 4:00 A.M. with breakfast, going to PT, a five-mile run, and then reporting for work. We all had our individual jobs. Some worked in the motor pool as mechanics, some were aircraft mechanics in the aviation section, or weather specialists, and then there were the gofers.

Most of the time there was some Sergeant yelling at somebody for something they considered stupid. "You're a sorry looking trooper" or "get your head out of your ass and do something right for a change" were a couple of the insults hurled at us. So, naturally whenever we had a chance to either get away or to get away with something, we did.

Every now and then we would have inspections. The inspections were spot checks to see if the men and equipment were in a readied state for combat. We were always preparing for readiness...constant shit! We were notified 24 hours before an inspection. That meant we would have to work all night to make sure everything was in a combat-ready condition.

Once during one of these stateside inspections, Peterson's jeep had no water in the radiator. He swore that someone sabotaged his jeep. Well, with no water in sight and his jeep next in line for inspection, he found a container of clear fluid on the floor, and poured it into his radiator without knowing what it was. When the inspection team went through his jeep, the conversation went wild.

Inspector, "Hey why is there smoke coming out of that radiator? Is it hot"?

The second inspector, "No it's not hot to the touch."

First inspector: "Let's take a look."

Second inspector: "Shit! This shit looks like battery acid. Who the fuck put battery acid in the radiator? Whose jeep is this?"

I turned to Peterson, "Hey, Pete, I think you're up shits creek this time. You better hope the BC is in a good mood."

We always pulled some kind of nonsense like that. During the same type of inspection, a team would generally go through everyone's locker to check uniforms and other items for neatness. I happened to have a woman's see through nightie in my locker. I was planning to send it home to my girl.

"Pete, watch this shit. I'm going to hang it up in my locker along with my uniforms. They'll go ape-shit."

"Russo, where the fuck is Russo?" The first Sergeant was screaming for me.

Pete, "Hey Russo, I think you're up the creek now."

As I entered the barracks, the First Sergeant couldn't wait for me to get in before he started to lay into me.

"Russo, what the fuck do you call this? Do you wear this to bed at night?" Captain Goodbolt to Sergeant, "he knows better than to pull this shit."

Captain Goodbolt, "Russo, what is this shit? Are you doing this just to piss off the First Sergeant or what?"

"Well Sir, I said, that is part of my personal wardrobe. It's not against regulations to have civilian clothes even if it is a bit feminine, sir."

Captain Goodbolt, "Well, First Sergeant, he's got you there."

The first Sergeant was pissed. He looked at me and said, "We're not done with this shit, Russo. Get this out of your locker!"

CHAPTER 7

We called them "90 day wonders" or "bar fucks". They used to say that if you worked your ass off for 90 days, you could do nothing for the rest of your life. It was a slight exaggeration, but that sounded good to me...no more work for the rest of my time in the military. OK, sounded too good, but the thing I wanted most was to take it a little easier.

I wish I had known how the military worked before I joined, because I would have done things very differently. I would have negotiated a better deal before I enlisted. I learned the hard way, but now I knew what had to be done, and I did not want to waste any more time.

It wasn't until I climbed to the enlisted rank of E5 Sergeant, that the Army decided that they were going to put out a call for aviation personnel. That sucked because once we received E-5 status, life became easier. We were giving more orders now than we were receiving, and we were the ones calling other guys 'shit heads' and 'fuck-ups. Our lot had improved significantly, but I still wasn't satisfied.

The aviation program was given a big push because the army needed aviation people very badly; so badly they actually changed the entrance examination and training time for the program.

I can remember the day they posted the bulletin. I could hear Peterson halfway down the hall.

"Are you shitting me? Where do I sign? This program is just what the doctor ordered!"

A bell went off in our heads; a chance to work toward our common goal of 'no more work', or at least that's what we thought. It seemed that all we had to do was pass a test. We scrambled to call in our markers. First we hit Guillardo, the Company Clerk.

"Hey, Guillardo, do you have the forms we need to apply for this new school?"

Guillardo "Hey, guys, don't crowd me. Let me find out what the prerequisites are. You know if you don't have certain scores, you can't get in."

Peterson... "Ya Ya, just find out what we have to do and fix it. Come on, Guillardo, we know you can do it."

Pete was baiting him like you would a little boy. Guillardo would act as though he didn't like it, but really thoroughly enjoyed that kind of kidding around. I always thought that he was a bit on the feminine side, but I always figured if he were gay he wouldn't be in a paratroop unit. What did I know?

"Guillardo, see if you can call some of your clerk friends and get us a copy of the test."

"Look you guys; I can't do that."

Pete, "Why not. You owe us; we know you can do it. Come on Guillardo."

Guillardo, kind of kidding back, said, Ok, Ok you guys, but you're going to get me into a lot of trouble one of these days. I'll get it for you, but you better not screw me up. Once you have it, I don't know where you got it. Understand?"

"Ok, Guillardo, you had nothing to do with it, when do we get it? How about tomorrow?"

"Russo, I said I'd get it as soon as I can...gees."

Peterson, "No more walking. Flying is the way to go!"

Vietnam was the sole reason the Army had to increase the numbers in Army aviation. The war had started to escalate, and the military was utilizing helicopters as their principal means of transport to fight that war. Our unit had an aviation section assigned to it for artillery support made up of a few pilots and mechanics. There weren't many aircraft in our section, but we still viewed it as a sign that things were finally looking up for us. It looked like we were finally going to have a chance to advance.

The notice said they were seeking applicants for aviation personnel, and were giving preference to those who had an understanding of aircraft and any knowledge of aviation. Written tests and a stringent flight physical would be given to those who applied. If by some chance we passed, we would become trainees in the program. Of course, visions of grandeur clouded our minds. We never gave a thought to the reason the Army wanted more trained aviation members, Vietnam. I know now that we were a bit shortsighted.

CHAPTER 8

We never understood the meaning of "stay out of trouble". Probably because we equated trouble with fun. Perhaps it was something inside each and every paratrooper that caused us to chase after excitement and adventure. That something that often put us over the edge; filled us with feelings of immortality; allowing us to think, "It will never happen to us"; that put a little bit of devil in each of us.

When I think about our Friday escapades at the Shauny Town Bar; stepping into harm's way; mixing with all sorts of rough characters, and thinking it was fun. Today, I wouldn't even walk into a place like that. It didn't matter who or why we fought. Hormones raged and adrenaline rushed, and so we fought.

Military life in the 60's was constant drinking, fighting, chasing women and training for our next combat mission, but not necessarily in that order. We were young, energetic, and sometimes driven by our raging hormones trying to pack a lot living into every day. The Army never discouraged our drinking and questionable off-hour pursuits. Who knows what motivated the Army. Was it because they understood only too well what lay ahead of us? I do know that boredom and loneliness were the culprits that enticed us to drink so much, and then do things that we would not normally do if we were home with family and friends. Drinking and craziness were our coping mechanisms. Everyone has their own way of dealing with situations.

There was this one fellow named Guy who had his own unique way of coping. When Guy was low on cash or had nothing to do, he would go down and hop a freight train, and didn't get off until the train stopped or the weekend was over. He was kind of a shady character. He wasn't like the rest of our group. It's my belief that he was encouraged to join the military by a judge who gave him a choice, either join or go to jail.

"Hey, Russo, what are you doing this weekend? I know that the other guys went on leave. Are you going to hang around the barracks all weekend?"

"I don't know Guy. What's on your mind?"

"Well, I have a girlfriend going to college up in Bowling Green, Kentucky, and she's having a party. She just called, and told me to come up and bring some friends."

Guy was one of those people who really didn't have friends because nobody trusted him. However, he was very resourceful. He had a very persuasive way about him. He had a way of producing things you needed and money never changed hands. I personally didn't trust him, but he could be interesting to have around.

"Look, Guy, I would go, but it's raining like hell and unless you have a car, I am not going to get soaked for a college party."

"Hey, Russo, if I can get us a ride off post, then a nice dry ride to Bowling Green, would you come?"

He was using his persuasive tactics on me. There should have been warning bells going off in my head, but instead I heard myself say, "I guess I would. It beats hanging around here all weekend."

We went to the parking lot and one of the Sergeants was just about ready to go off post. Guy asked, more like begged, for a ride to just outside the post gates and that is exactly where we were unceremoniously dumped.

"Get your sorry asses out of my vehicle, and start humping down the highway."

The gate MP told us, "You two sorry fucks are going to get soaked."

We were dropped off on the wrong side of the highway, and trying to get across almost got us killed.

"Russo, don't look at me that way, just follow me and we'll be out of this weather in a couple of minutes."

I was already getting pissed because it was pelting rain, and the skies were as dark as they could possibly be without it being night. It was so cold we could see our breath as we talked; the rain was getting heavier; and the sound of passing vehicles all but drowned out most of our conversation.

Guy led me to a railroad crossing. The arms came down to stop the traffic, and the train started to cross the highway.

Guy, "Come on, Russo. This is the nice dry ride I promised you. The train goes real slow here so we can jump on."

At first I thought he was out of his mind, but after thinking it over I decided, what the hell, I didn't have anything better to do. To be honest, I felt like a kid again doing something I knew I wasn't supposed to do. So I followed Guy through an opened boxcar door, and off we went into the night. It was pitch black out. We rode along the countryside and there were no lights anywhere. We couldn't see roads or anything so after a half hour or so, I dozed off to sleep.

We were awakened by a sudden jerk of the boxcar accompanied by loud banging noises. Suddenly we realized we had stopped.

"Don't worry, Russo, we'll start moving again soon."

I looked out of the freight car and saw what looked like a cornfield. A little further off in the distance was a farmhouse with a light of some kind illuminating a small road. I lit a cigarette. Again, another big bang and a jerking of the cars. I heard the engine up ahead moving along the track. I heard lots of noise up front where the engine was, but nothing back where we were. I couldn't believe it, the damn engine left without us. We were stuck out in the middle of nowhere. We didn't have a clue where we were. I knew I shouldn't have trusted Guy!

The rain had subsided a little.

"Well, Guy, we're stuck out here. Now what do we do shit head?"

"I don't know. I never had this problem before, but I'll figure something out."

We decided to make our way through the soaking wet cornfield heading toward the farmhouse. After a 45-minute walk that left us drenched to the bone, we hit asphalt. Hallelujah! Now all we had to do was find out where the hell we were.

We were on a two-lane road that was dotted by street lamps. Cornfields lined both sides of the road, and an occasional farmhouse could be seen. After walking and hitchhiking about ten miles or so we came across a roadside bar with a few cars parked outside. Guy told me he was going inside to take a leak.

I told him, "I'll be walking down the road hitchhiking. When you're done, catch up to me. If I get a ride, I'll try to wait for you." We agreed. After walking about a thousand yards, a car pulled up to me and stopped.

The driver, "where are you going? Need a lift soldier?"

I knew that voice. It was Guy, and that bastard had a car.

"Where the hell did you get this car?" I asked.

"Oh, back at the bar", Guy said, "The keys were in the ignition, so I took it. Jump in. Let's go!"

I couldn't believe it. I guess everything I had heard about him was true. He was a bit of a trouble maker. After we had driven through a couple of towns, I was getting a little nervous.

"Look, Guy, when we get to the next town I want to dump this thing. I don't like this at all."

He agreed, and so at the next town we left the car on a back street. We parked it on a well-lit street, and walked away. I felt a lot easier then. I wasn't up for experiencing the hospitality of a southern jail.

After unloading the car, we made our way to the main road; stopped at a gas station to find out where we were; and started hitch hiking once again. As luck would have it, it started to rain again. How great was my life? Of course with the rain came the penetrating cold chilling me to the bone.

After we walked for a mile, a car full of college kids pulled over and gave us a ride. The driver asked if we were as soaked as we looked. We were worse than we looked.

"I'll put the heater on for you guys. Maybe that will help."

The heat felt so good. Soon after I took off my wet coat, and I fell asleep. Suddenly Guy started shaking me to wake up. It was already time to get out. I swear it felt like I had just closed my eyes, but a good hour must have gone by.

Guy, "all we need to do is walk a couple of miles, bang a right, and we're there."

"We're where?" I asked.

"Where? At my girl's house."

We walked for what seemed like forever, and then came to a house with a broken storm door. It was missing glass, and apparently springs as well because the wind kept blowing it open banging it against the house. The house was dark with the only light coming from a streetlight out front. The street was quiet, except for the incessant banging of the door, and the rain had finally stopped, for the moment anyway. My teeth were chattering because I was so wet and cold. Guy banged on the door several times.

I asked, "Are you sure we're at the right house? Maybe they're just not home?"

Before Guy could answer me, I heard the latch start to jiggle, and the door opened. There stood a pixie-like brunette, wearing an extra-long t-shirt. She A looked like she had just tumbled out of bed. Guy asked if Sherry was home.

He said, "She wasn't expecting me, but I decided to surprise her."

She looked us over for a few seconds and said, "She's not in. I don't know when she will be back, but you guys can come in and wait if you want." She stared at me for a few seconds, "you look like you're soaked. Come in and get warm."

She was speaking with the cutest little drawl. When we entered the house, we passed by the front room; a room that would normally be the living room had two sets of bunk beds.

I asked her, "how many people live here? It looks like you have a barracks set up here."

She said, "Just me and a few other girls sharing the rent, it beats living in dorm."

She directed us into the middle room where a TV was on and corner lights were dimly lit.

"You guys can help yourselves to some beer in the fridge if you like. Why don't you take off your wet clothes? I have some blankets you can use while your clothes are drying."

Guy, "Hey, what's your name? I hate getting undressed in front of people when I don't know their name."

"Go into the bathroom, and get undressed if you're that shy. I wasn't looking for a show, you know."

"That's O.K., if you'd like a show we'll do one for you. By the way, what did you say your name was?"

She introduced herself, "I'm Carol, and the girl sleeping in that other chair is Linda. I know who you are. You're the Army guy that Sherry goes out with. I've heard all about you."

Guy sat back in the couch and said, "And I've heard all about you." She snickered and shook her head.

We went into the bathroom and got undressed. The bathroom looked like it hadn't been cleaned in months. Clothes were hanging all over the place.

Guy yelling, "Hey, is it alright if we put on these nice dry panties?"

Carol came charging in, "Give me that underwear." She paused for a few seconds; Guy had already stripped and I wasn't far behind.

After she took a long look, she said, "and I'll take those bras too."

I said, "You should be ashamed of yourself wearing bras in this day and age. I've heard no self-respecting college student would be caught dead in a bra. Aren't you into protesting?" She said nothing. She just reached out and grabbed the remaining underwear. She went into the other room, but left the bathroom door open. Removing my underwear, I turned in time to see both girls watching.

"So you two are interested in a show."

Linda, "Do you guys work out?"

I guess we were in pretty good shape from all of the exercise we had to do. I wrapped the small blanket around me, picked up my clothes, and headed into the kitchen placing them on chairs by the stove to dry.

"No, we just do a lot of heavy work. It keeps us in shape."

As I walked back into the room, I could see up under Carol's T-shirt, since she had her feet up on the coffee table making it easy for everyone except a blind man to see that she was wearing white panties that didn't quite conceal the dark hair beneath. She was rolling a joint, and asked if we would like some.

Guy, "Hell, Ya. I could go for some. How about you, Russo?"

"OK", she said, "I'll light it for you, then pass it around."

Guy turned and whispered, "We're going to get balled tonight! These two are going to do a number on us. I've heard about them from Sherry. They are wild."

Most guys would love to be in this situation, but to be honest, I was feeling a little uncomfortable. First, the blanket kept falling off of me because it really wasn't big enough. And every time I moved the wrong way I revealed more of me than I had intended. The girls thought it was funny. Secondly, I really didn't like to smoke pot. I had tried it before, and it didn't do much for me. I really didn't care for the way it made me feel.

After a few puffs on the joint, Guy got up, walked straight over to Linda, dropped his blanket and slipped his hand down the outside of her t-shirt and squeezed one of her breasts. She stood up and they kissed. It was that easy. When he reached down and slid off her panties, she started to protest.

He said, "Shut the fuck up. Let's go into the bedroom." He grabbed her, and nudged her into the direction of the bedroom. I could hear him saying, "How about a little head? Come on, I know you love it. Get down there."

I thought, what the hell, so I slid over toward Carol, reached out and did the same.

She said, "Do you want any more of this joint?"

I shook my head no. She got up to crush it out. As she was doing that, I slid her panties down to reveal a perfectly round, plump ass. These girls had great bodies. I couldn't wait to get started.

She protested, "Stop, not here. Let's go to my bed."

OK, I thought, show me the way. Well her bed just happened to be one of the upper bunks.

"How are we supposed to get it on up there?"

She put her hand over my mouth.

"If you climb up there, I'll show you."

It seemed like she had done this before, because she was up and on top of me in seconds. She lowered herself down on me, kissed me.

Carol, "that feels great, soldier, just keep on going. After some time went by she asked, "Do you think you can continue?" What a question? I looked into her eyes. "Hmm, you know it."

I don't remember when it ended. I fell asleep, and was awakened by the sun shining through a window. Carol was not in bed with me, but as I looked across the room I could see Linda's naked body lying on the other bed. Now that's the way I like to wake up in the morning.

I was still naked, and a little cold so I went off toward the kitchen to look for my clothes. As I walked through the middle room, I ran into Carol watching TV still wearing that same T-shirt. There was another girl sitting with her, but she was fully dressed. As I walked by naked as a jaybird, I said, "Hi-hello-what's happening? I'm just going to find my clothes." The other girl gave me a big smile, and then she turned to Carol.

"Hmm, Carol, I see what you mean."

They both began laughing. When I reached the kitchen my clothes were still a little wet. The two girls followed close behind.

Carol, "We were going to make some breakfast. Do you want some? Don't get dressed yet, your clothes are still wet. If you wait, I'll iron them for you so they'll dry faster."

I was getting embarrassed standing there naked. It's one thing to be naked and going at it, but I felt uncomfortable just standing there being stared at.

"Look, I need to get dressed. I'm not going to just stand around like this until my clothes dry."

"Well", she said, "it's not like I haven't seen it before. How about a blanket or towel or something".

The other girl had a look on her face like she was starved, and I was her next meal. She said to Carol, "I don't know, Carol, I kind of like him like this. What do you think?"

I told them that I wouldn't mind staying undressed if they took off all of their clothes too.

She said, "I feel OK the way I am, but I wouldn't mind if we got a little closer so you can warm up.

I started taking off her clothes while thinking to myself that this is much too easy. I must have landed in a whorehouse. The girls back home sure didn't behave like this.

Then I felt Carol's arms slide around me, and work her way down my thighs. One hand started to work its way back up between them. The other girl was still undressing, but paused for a moment, bent over and took me into her mouth. Her warm, wet mouth and lips caressed me. She was very good at this. I felt like my legs were going to crumble under me. Finally, that free love everyone had been talking about. What a great idea! Oops—don't stop, honey. Keep going—I love you too—flower power and all of that shit. The two of them were incredible.

Eventually, it had to end. I never did get to meet Sherry, but her roommates more than made up for it.

Later that morning we all decided to go to lunch.

Guy said, "I am buying everyone lunch. Do you girls know a good place?"

Carol said she knew of one, and then we were off. I was really shocked that Guy offered to buy lunch for everyone. That type of gesture just didn't seem like his style, but I wasn't about to look a gift horse in the mouth.

The restaurant wasn't great. It was a typical college town burger joint. Burgers, chili dogs and spaghetti, all of the great foods. Gourmet it wasn't, but we were so hungry, that it didn't matter. We all ordered burgers, beer and fries. Everything was going great until Guy nudged me and whispered.

"I don't have any money."

I almost choked on my burger, literally. I gave him an 'I don't believe it' look.

He said, "When I tell you to bolt, then go with me out the door."

Again I gave him a dirty look. I wasn't going to do it. I shook my head. After finishing his meal, he stood up from the table, and said he had to go to the rest room. He never came back.

After 10 minutes the girls started to realize something was wrong.

"Where the fuck is your friend?" one of them asked. "Was he ever intending to pay for this meal?"

Look girls, I said, I don't know what happened to him. I have a couple of bucks, and if you girls can throw some money in with me, I'm sure we can get

After the bill was paid, the girls gave me a piece of their mind.

"Thanks a lot for nothing. Don't you guys ever come back here again! You're two fuck'n assholes as far as we're concerned."

I never went back there except in dreams. A guy never forgets a weekend like that.

CHAPTER 9

Most airborne divisions were dismantled after the Second World War. In the 60's the only divisions that remained active were the 82^{nd,} the 101st and some minor brigades like the 173rd infantry. The 82nd and the 101st were both considered strategic combat divisions. That meant they were always combat ready to go anywhere in the world to fight in a minimum amount of time. My understanding was that they were responsible for covering the world's hot spots.

In the mid 1960's our unit, like many others, was put on alert. They didn't tell us where we were going, but we all had a feeling that this was not a training exercise. We boarded an aircraft with full combat gear in the middle of the night with thousands of other troops. We found out later that this was the beginning of the war between Egypt and Israel. The United States was preparing to use parachute divisions, in the event they would be needed; and we were told that the Russians were also in the air, and vowing their support to Egypt. It could have been the start of another World War. Here we are some 30+ years later, and the truth of what could have happened has never been told.

Another operation that was never revealed to the American public was when Castro started problems at Guantanimo Bay in Cuba. At briefings, we were told that the US was going to invade Cuba. We were in Florida at one of the military airports occupying several runways for several days waiting for the seventh fleet to move into position. The Marines were going to invade through an amphibious assault to the south, and we were to parachute into the North. By the time the fleet got into position, the politicians negotiated with Castro and the action was placed on hold.

In early 1967, several others and I were notified that we were accepted into aviation school. The orders came directing us to report to Fort Eustis, Virginia, for TDY (Temporary Duty). When the TDY orders arrived, I knew I was going to return to the 101st when I was done with Aviation School. That was good news, because it meant I would be coming back to serve with my friends.

I decided to travel to Virginia on my motorcycle. I had purchased a motorcycle from a soldier who was discharged. He wasn't going to ship it home because of the cost, so he sold me the machine for $350. I borrowed the money because I had to have that bike. I needed transportation. My main financial backer was a soldier who had recently returned from Vietnam with heavy head injuries. That's probably why he lent me the money. Frank was a grunt, a ground soldier. He and his squad were caught in an ambush by Vietcong guerillas, and he was shot in the head. The Army gave him a steel plate, and allowed him to take it easy until his discharge papers were processed. Frank was one of many who "saw the light". He had tons of money because he spent the last couple of years in Vietnam and in the hospital. His pay was sent home for him. I asked him if I could borrow the money.

He said, "Take all you want. I've decided to change my ways. I'm still alive, and that's all that counts. I've been given a second chance at life, and money doesn't mean that much to me anymore."

Frank was a good man, especially since he lent me the money.

As I tied my duffel bag onto my motorcycle, it started to rain, naturally. Of course, I didn't check the weather before planning this trip. The rain followed me for two days. On top of the weather my motorcycle was having clutch problems. The damn thing wouldn't disengage which meant I had to try and synchronize my shifting, without a clutch, to the engine's intermittent revs. When I had to stop at a light, I would lie back and downshift to first gear and hope that the light would change before I had to stop. If stopping was essential. I would shift into neutral. To start going again, I had to get off the bike and push it fast enough to drop it into first gear on a roll. The bike would buck a little. Then as I increased speed, it would smooth out again. Driving without a clutch was a bitch. Imagine doing that for a few hundred miles through small southern towns.

When I reached Roanoke Virginia, while passing through an intersection, was struck by a semi-tractor trailer hauling a full load of furniture. The truck hit me with its left front wheel. The fender hooked onto the bike frame dragging me and the motorcycle about a block before coming to a full stop. I was lucky it was raining. Back in the sixties there were no helmet laws. Therefore, bikers didn't wear helmets, unless it was raining. My helmet had a plastic face guard that kept the rain from my face. After the accident, I noticed my helmet had a deep gouge on the side, with the truck's paint embedded in it. That would have been my head if it weren't for the rain.

After all of the noise had stopped, I found myself on my back looking up at the sky. My motorcycle had landed on top of me, and the hot engine was beginning to burn my leg. There was a crowd of people gathered around the scene looking at me lying there helpless, but none of them offered any assistance. The shit heads, it was a good thing that the engine wasn't on fire, or I would have been up "shits creek" again. Eventually, one man came up beside me, and asked if he could help. I told him to get the bike off me fast. He did, and I was grateful for that stranger's help.

He said "If you need a witness, I was in Red's Bar, over there. I saw the whole thing."

Unfortunately, the police never canvassed the area for witnesses. I was taken to a local hospital to have my leg x-rayed. They found that the leg bone wasn't broken even though I could hardly move it. While I was waiting to be taken for x-rays, I noticed that one of the nurses was paying more attention to me than was necessary. She seemed real interested, and I loved every minute of it. When we were alone, she talked about my injuries, and hinted at how awkward it would be to become intimate with that bad leg. At first I thought she was just making small talk, joking around, and was just being nice trying to boost my ego.

She was a pretty little thing. She was petite with red hair, about 5' 4" and talked with the most adorable drawl. Actually, all of the southern girls had the most adorable little drawl. When she helped me into the wheel chair, she placed her arms around my waist, and asked me, rather seductively, if she was hurting my leg. I told her not to worry about my leg, that if she found us an empty room, I could show her just how well I could operate with that bad leg. I figured she would tell me to drop dead, give me a little slap or have a different nurse take me to x-ray. I had nothing to lose. Instead, she glanced up and down the hall to see if anyone was coming, then she leaned over and firmly gave me a kiss on the mouth. I was so surprised I didn't know what to say or do.

"It's after 3:00, and most of the workers have gone home. Can you really operate with that leg as well as you say or are you just bragging?"

I smiled as she leaned over me and started pushing the chair down the hall and into an empty room. The room looked like it wasn't used much, but came equipped with a cushioned examining table in the center. She smiled as she helped me up onto it.

She said, "Relax Hon, I'll do all the work. When I'm done with you, your leg won't bother you at all. Wherever you go or whomever you're with, you'll never forget me!" She started with my pants, and had me completely stripped within a few seconds. She climbed up onto the table with me, and lifted her white skirt unveiling white nylons. Some women back then still wore garter belts and she was one of them. She conveniently wasn't wearing any panties to hide that gorgeous red mound. Ah, a true redhead! I reached up and started to rub her legs. She immediately stopped me.

"I told you, you're not to do a thing. I'll do all of the work."

She meant business, and I didn't mind. She did things to my young body that I had never experienced before, and it was a long time before I experienced it again. Not only was she gorgeous, but very skillful. When she was done with me, I laid sexually exhausted and satisfied. She helped me get dressed and pushed me back to the main room. She told me that she had to leave, and that someone else would take over. I asked if I could see her later that night. She had agreed to come by and see me before her shift was over. I waited for her, but she never came back, and I never saw her again. From time to time I might see a petite redhead and immediately think of her. I guess the experience was just that, an experience.

As I was waiting for the doctor to tell me if there were any real problems, I overheard voices in the hall asking the doctor if the patient, Russo, could be released. The doctor told them that there weren't any major problems, therefore I could be released. The inquisitors were police officers apparently waiting to haul me away. One walked into the room.

"Let's go. The doctor said you can be released, and the judge is waiting in court for you."

I had heard of kangaroo courts in the South, but this was unbelievable. I asked them what they meant by the judge waiting in court.

One said, "It's 4:30 on Friday. Court usually closes at 4:30, but the judge wants to hear this case before you and that truck driver have a chance to skip town."

I said, "This was only an accident. What case?"

He just pointed towards the door, and gestured for me to go. I wasn't really in a great position or condition to argue with them.

When I entered the Court, I was escorted to the front of the room. A Bailiff asked me to give him my driver's license and motorcycle registration. He took the documents, and brought them to the Judge's bench. I looked up to see them having quite a discussion. Every now and then they would turn and look at me like I had two heads. I was beginning to get a strange sinking feeling in the pit of my stomach.

The judge, "is the truck driver here?"

"I'm here, your honor." He continued, "your honor, I have been driving for sixty odd years, and ain't never had an accident in all that time."

The judge barked, "I didn't ask you how long you have been driving, now did I? When I want information from you, I'll ask you for it. Now sit down."

The Bailiff was standing next to me, "How the hell old is this guy if he's been driving for sixty years? The bastard must be in his seventies."

The Judge barked again, "I want silence in this court room, Mr. Russell, do you understand me?"

I answered "yes, your honor." Part of me wanted to say, "Russo, your honor", but I thought it was best to let it go.

"Mr. Russell, approach the bench!"

When I reached the bench, he started to talk.

"Please explain to me, number one, why your driver's license is two years expired; number two, your vehicle registration says Tennessee; and your number plate is from Kentucky. Please explain and don't take all night."

Before I had a chance to talk, the Judge impatiently turned to the truck driver.

"What color was the light when you went through the intersection and struck Mr. Russell?"

The old man said, "Green, and I didn't see him until I hit him."

I then spoke up, "his light was red, and he went right through it, your honor."

The judge looked at me long and hard.

"Mr. Russell, do you want to leave this court room a free man tonight?"

I said, "Yes, you're Honor."

"Then shut your mouth. I don't know, and I don't care why your license has been expired for two years or why your number plates are in the state they are, but I'll tell you this, you are lucky you're in the military; just passing through; and its Friday afternoon. Now, Mr. Russell, when did you first see the truck, and make it brief."

"Well, your Honor, I first saw the truck when it was about a foot from my leg, and my light was green."

The judge just shook his head.

"Boy, I didn't ask you what color the light was, now did I?"

Before I could answer, he pounded the gavel on the bench and said, "I find both parties guilty of negligent driving. Mr. Russell, I am not going to fine you because of your injuries, but you, pointing to the truck driver, will pay a $100 fine, case dismissed."

The police escorted me down the stairs, into a cruiser, and off to the bus terminal. Time wise, I was lucky. The next bus to the Fort Eustis area was only a couple of hours wait. As I strolled into the bus terminal with the two police officers, most of the people in the bus terminal were staring at me. The police carried my belongings to the ticket window. It looked as though they were telling me to get out of town. My motorcycle was completely demolished. I would have to make arrangements later about the bike. I was a little relieved. Driving all that way in the rain had taken its toll on me. I was ready for a relaxing ride on the bus.

Fort Eustis was the home of another newly formed Flight Training Center. Normally it was the home of the Army Transportation Center. They usually trained mechanics for aviation, ships piloting or vehicle transportation. The base, located close to Virginia Beach, was in a great location for summer fun, and I had planned on having myself a blast here.

The base transportation dropped me off at my training unit for billeting. I was supposed to sign in wearing a uniform. As I entered the building, I noticed a couple of guys hanging out of the window. They were soldiers that had just come out of boot camp, and were sent for advanced training to the Transportation Center.

One soldier said to the other, "Looks like we have a new recruit coming in. Let's give him the business."

"Hey", one yelled to me, "recruits are not allowed to enter through that door."

The other person started, "y'all stand at attention when you're spoken too!"

I was wearing civilian clothes, but my jacket had a round patch on it that said, United States Paratrooper with a picture of a parachute in the middle. I gave them a long, cold stare, and said nothing. They must have seen the patch on the jacket because they disappeared. The driver, helping me with my bags laughingly said, "They must have realized that they said the wrong thing to the wrong person. They certainly took off real fast."

Having an advanced rank provided privileges during training that other candidates did not enjoy. The other aviation school trainees were subject to many disciplinary actions designed to keep them under control, while I was free to roam the base.

One of the privileges we enjoyed was a private room instead of sleeping in a squad room. However, there was one drawback. Two of the men in training were from the country of Guatemala. Our government decided that these two needed to be chaperoned and kept out of trouble. So, they decided I was to be their baby sitter. They both spoke English well enough. I just couldn't figure out why they needed watching.

The night we were introduced they wanted to go for drinks at the NCO (Non Commissioned Officers) club on base. I really didn't want to go out, but they insisted.

"Come on you Paratroopi, let's go."

Their nickname for me was Troopa, Troopa, Paratroopa it was said in sing-song fashion.

There were many married woman at the club who came by themselves. Their husbands were sent to Vietnam, and they were left behind living on post. Some of these women were left alone for over a year. Need I say more? For the two Latinos, it was like taking a kid into a candy store.

After a couple of hours in the club, they were on their way home with a couple of these women.

I told them, "whatever you do, get your asses back to the barracks before daybreak or the brass will have my ass, comprende?"

They were two hot shits, and I had a lot of fun with them. They told me if I ever went to Guatemala for a visit, I must stop in and see them. I asked how I would find them?

One answered, "You come to airport, and we will be there."

I said, "Hey, with all of the Air Force stationed at that airport, how am I going to find you two?"

"Paratroopa, it's easy. We only have four airplanes in our Air Force. You come to hanger, and ask for us."

They were characters, and their unique perspective always provided a good laugh.

Spending weekends at Virginia Beach, visiting Williamsburg and the historic surroundings made the training more than enjoyable. The best part of being in the area though was meeting Pam. She was tall and slim with long blonde hair.

One night I decided to venture off post heading toward a couple of local towns looking for a little excitement. My totaled motorcycle meant that I was reduced to hitchhiking. I was picked up by a couple of local yahoos, who told me about a quaint little town near the seashore. They dropped me off near a small diner where I decided to warm my bones with a cup of coffee. That's when I noticed her. She was so beautiful. I asked for coffee, and she obliged with a sweet smile.

I was trying to get up enough nerve to ask her if she would meet me after she finished work. I didn't know what I would do if she said yes, because I didn't have a car, and it was very cold outside. I nursed the coffee for close to an hour just looking at her, not knowing how to make the next move. She must have sensed what I was thinking, because she came over smiling.

She said, "I noticed you watching me, do you have something on your mind?"

I was so embarrassed; all I could do was smile back.

"Let me help you. I get off work at 11:30. Since you don't have a car, (she smiled) I noticed, don't worry, I do. Is this making any sense to you?"

I said, "Absolutely."

"If you would like, you can wait in my car, and I'll see you when I get off at 11:30,"

I thought I had died and gone to heaven. What luck! I couldn't wait. The clock seemed to drag on, but finally it was 11:30. She came out from the diner wearing a big smile. She saw me sitting there waiting for her.

"I'm happy I offered, and so glad you waited."

We talked for a few minutes, and then decided to go for a couple of drinks. The chemistry between us was definitely working. I didn't have much money, which wasn't anything new. I certainly didn't want to ask her to pay, so I suggested that we go out to a nice quiet area to talk, and she agreed. But, all of the time, in the back of my mind, I just wanted to jump her bones.

She drove down a quaint little brick road. As she was driving, I was taking in the scenery, mostly her. She stopped in a little local park. She noted that nobody goes there in the winter, and how perfect it would be for us to talk. We talked about her last boyfriend who was in the Marines, and went back home. She didn't feel that he was the one for her so, when he left for home without her, she really didn't mind. The talk also turned to my military career. I told her that I knew it was inevitable that I was going to Vietnam, and I had heard rumors that my Division was being sent over. It would happen about the time I finished my training.

It was beginning to feel a little cold sitting there in the car so I offered her my jacket. As we touched slightly I could feel a tingling in my body. Being young, I always reacted on impulse. When our eyes grew close, we kissed. Kissing became touching, and then somehow we ended up in the back seat.

Her scent was overwhelming, and before we knew it we were making love, love as passionate as I have ever known. We were unable to keep our hands off each other all night. Our relationship was so thrilling it continued into every free moment I had. Day or night, that's all I could think of, was her. She taught me how to love, and what it felt like to be loved by a knowing woman. I think at that tender age I became a more sensitive lover from the experience we shared over those several weeks.

Unfortunately, we met when I was just about to finish training. Pam and I continued seeing each other as much as possible. Her parents were not especially happy with her seeing another military person. It seemed her last boyfriend, the Marine, caused havoc with her home life turning them against all service men. He had made many promises to her and her family that he had no intention of keeping.

I could understand why they were less than cordial toward me. Of course, I knew that there would never be any future for Pam and me. I think she felt the same way. At least that's what I told myself. We had this passion that we had to deal with. We just enjoyed each other while we could.

A short time later I received notice from Headquarters Div-Arty that we were going over. The 101st Division was packing and preparing for deployment. The other guys from my unit were slightly delayed in reporting to Virginia. Of course, when they finally arrived it was party time.

CHAPTER 10

Soon Pete and a couple of the other guys arrived on base. The trip to Virginia with these guys wouldn't be the same without some sort of incident happening, and of course it didn't take long before one did. The first night Pete and the guys arrived, we decided to go off post and have a few drinks. We stopped for beer in the first package store we came across. After all, we needed a couple to keep us going until we found a bar.

When we stopped at the liquor store, Pete started talking to a couple of local girls who invited us to their house for a party. When we arrived at the house the girls wanted to hear all about the military. We always loved to tell our *war* stories. This was too good to be true, an audience just dying to hear all about us brave paratroopers.

In the middle of one of our stories the front door flew open, and banged back against the wall. In came five local guys who were obviously more familiar with the girls than we were. We were still in our fatigues, and they commented on the "chicken" located on our shoulders. They were referring to the Screaming Eagle patch we wore. An argument ensued, and before we knew it, one of our guys placed his wallet on the table and bet the locals that he could climb up to the roof, jump off, and not get hurt. They accepted the bet and up he went. Both Pete and myself tried to stop him, but he was so drunk that he wouldn't listen. He made the climb, not too steady, weaving back and forth a little, and jumped.

I don't think I have ever seen anyone do as such a perfect parachute-landing fall as he did. I guess being drunk had its advantage. However, when it was time to pay up, the locals refused and a fight began. One of the locals had a steel pipe, and hit our jumper on the head rendering him unconscious. The medics came and rushed him to the hospital, but it was too late. He was pronounced dead on arrival at the hospital. He was such a young person, married and with a small child. This was one of the few times he was away from his wife, and just wanted to have a good time. It was a stupid tragedy. We think of him often.

Before we were finished with our training we were officially notified that the 101st Division in its entirety was going to Vietnam. This was to be the largest military airlift in the history of modern warfare. Since I was in Army Aviation, I found myself assigned to the advance party to Vietnam. My mission was to set up a heliport and maintenance operation for the main body following us over.

I said my goodbyes to Pam. She was a good person, and a wonderful companion to have when I was away from home. Sometimes you meet people in your life who are only meant to be there for a time. As young as we were, I think we both understood that.

On my return to Fort Campbell, I was immediately sent to work dismantling the aircraft for transporting to Vietnam. We swept the rotor blades back and installed transporting wheels to the skids of hueys for the move into the C-141's. Along with the aircraft there was a large variety of support equipment and parts, enough to last several months of operation.

Autumn was upon us and even in Kentucky it was beginning to get cold. I wanted to go home one more time before we had to depart for Vietnam. I requested, and was granted a ten day leave. When I returned home, I found that my friend who had joined the Air Force was also home on leave. It was a wonderful opportunity to let loose, and have a wild time.

I stopped by my girlfriend's house to become reacquainted. Her family owned a modest home in a town located just outside Boston's city limits. A large Italian population had settled in that area. They were mostly first and second generation. Her father was Italian, and had served with the invading U.S. forces in France. Her mother was French, and they met while he was serving there. Shortly thereafter, she became a war bride. They were well-respected people, and I liked them both.

Their daughter, Danielle, was my girl. She was gorgeous to look at, but also quiet and well liked. I knew from the first moment I saw her that she would be special. During that leave, if I wasn't spending time with her, I was with my buddy drinking, and doing crazy things like driving the beach surfing on the top of the car roof, in the middle of winter!

The ten days went by very fast. Before I knew it, I was at the airport saying good-by to Danielle and my family. They knew that when I returned to Kentucky I was going to be deployed to Vietnam. Trying to convince them that the time would go by fast, and that nothing would happen to me was not easy. How could I convince them that I wouldn't be coming home in a body bag like those they saw each evening on the news, when I didn't quite believe it myself? I tried to make them feel comfortable about the whole situation. I'm not sure I helped them. How could my simple words compete with the images on TV. Major General Barsonti, the Division Commander, accompanied by several of the General and Field Grade Officers, met us at the Ft. Campbell Army airfield to bid us a bon voyage and God speed as we headed for Vietnam. He walked through the ranks mingling with the men. He seemed to stop at every Italian he noticed, and talked to them like they were his peasants. I know because I was one of them.

After many hours of flying, we landed to refuel at an air base in San Franisco. We were given a short time to disembark and take a look around. The aircraft we were on carried our helicopters, pilots, and maintenance crew. Even though there was a lot of space in the aircraft, it was uncomfortable for such a long flight to Asia.

After refueling the next stop was to be somewhere in the pacific, Guam or Wake Island. It had been a long day, and we were beginning to tire from the hours of flying. The growing realization of where we were headed created a mixture of anticipation and anxiety that contributed to the effects of the long flight. I dozed, in that half asleep half-awake state for what seemed like hours until I was abruptly awakened by one of the men.

"I think the plane is on fire."

I took a look out of the window, then went to the pilot in command in the cockpit to find out what the hell was going on.

The pilot, with the rank of Major, replied, "Not to worry, one engine is giving us a little problem, but the fire is out now. We're at thirty-five thousand feet, and have plenty of room to play. I have some bad news though, we must change our flight plan and head for Hickem Field to repair the aircraft's engine."

We did not fully realize the ramification of that statement. As it happened, the airfield we were rerouted to was in the Hawaiian Islands. The Air Force, with all of their wisdom, decided to change engines instead of moving the cargo from one plane to another. The best part of this decision was that it would take two weeks to receive and install the new engine. For us it was party time. Two weeks of sun, booze, girls and booze again. It was a wild two weeks. We borrowed civilian clothes from some of the Air Force staff permanently assigned to the base, and had the time of our lives. The majority of the women we met were tourists, so for them it was also party time. Of course, they were feeling bad for the poor GI's that were going to Vietnam. They comforted us as much as possible. Though, I don't remember much of it, because I was in a constant state of drunkenness during those two weeks. The whole experience was nothing but a blur. I couldn't help thinking what the other guys were going to say when we told them about this situation.

CHAPTER 11

We arrived in-country early in the morning. It was still dark, and our landing was delayed due to a mortar attack on the Bien Hoi Airport. The whole atmosphere was different than anything we had previously experienced. The sky was completely illuminated by parachute flares. An aircraft called Puff was circling the airfield and randomly fired its retrofitted mini-guns.

A mini-gun is a modern version of a Gattlin Gun. It had several barrels that rotated by an electric motor, so that the barrels would stay cooler while firing some 7,000 rounds per minute. The red tracers could be seen for miles. The air smelled of burnt grass, and the airfield was a chaotic mass of activity. Although half asleep and somewhat weary from the long journey, I realized that I was witnessing the moment when my new world collided with the old, and that for at least the next year the country and home I left behind would be distant memories.

When I think back to that period in time, what I remember the most was our age. We were boys, boys who would become men much too soon. What we were about to experience shouldn't be experienced by anyone, at any age, let alone by mere boys. For those of us who survived the war, we may have survived physically in whole or in part, but we continue to fight it in the corners of our mind. Sometimes it overtakes us even now. Sometimes I feel like our youth was stolen from us, and we could never go back to recapture it because we were changed forever. That alone was a heavy price to pay.

The aircraft made its way into a bunker protected area. The cargo doors opened, and a Captain climbed into the rear of the aircraft.

He yelled, "All passengers are to enter the bus on the side of the road. Take your duffel bag with you when you depart. Please do so immediately."

After boarding the bus, the Captain started to sound off with authority.

"On behalf of MACV, the South Vietnamese Government, and the U.S. Army, I welcome you to Vietnam. We will be traveling approximately 25 miles to billeting. There you will meet other advance party members of the 101st. They will instruct you from there. Good Luck!"

Luck was what we needed. We were starting a journey that would change us forever. Emotions ranged from terror to rage. Wars caused by the out of control egos and mistakes of older men, have been waged by young men for centuries. Young men who should have been enjoying their youth, and creating prosperity, instead of sacrificing their precious commodities to protect these very men. Soldiers have always done their duty not merely to protect their government, but to safeguard their families and their way of life. Some become martyrs for freedom, admirable, but sad.

As the darkness started to slip into daylight, we could begin to make out small buildings constructed to house the troops in a base camp setting. This was our new world. A cold, unfamiliar place that we would inhabit for a very long time, or so it seemed.

We were dropped off at Div-arty. The "hooch" had a long flat concrete floor with cots located adjacent to each other. The roof was made of metal, and the windows were mosquito netted screens. Ceiling fans cast shadows on the walls as they thumped in rotation. We were given an opportunity to sleep for a couple of hours before we were acquainted with our duties.

The feeling of perspiration trickling down my face awakened me. There was a fan whirring above me, but the heat and humidity were too stifling for the fan to make much of a difference. I finally had to get up to find some cooler air, if that was possible. The heat was almost unbearable. I knew that my body would take time to adapt to this change in climate. I just hoped it wouldn't take too long to do it.

Later that day we were asked to drive down to the Div-Arty airfield, and set up for arriving aircraft. Once we arrived at the field we were reacquainted with a Sergeant named Pyatte. Pyatte was, for most of his military career, a mess hall cook. He was the most ornery person you could imagine. He was a mean son-of-a-bitch. Generally, we considered mess hall cooks or 'spoons, as we called them, as worthless, mean and nasty. When Pyatte decided to leave the kitchen and be retrained in the aircraft maintenance field, he acted no different. He was still as mean and ornery as anyone could be. All of the men hated him.

During those first few months, his men warned him that he needed to mend his ways or take a chance of being fragged. Fragging was a term used to describe a soldier who was killed by his own men. Once the men went as far as tossing a live grenade in his bunker. The pin was not pulled; it was a warning.

He had made a bunker at the bottom of the hill next to the maintenance tent. At the top of the hill was the motor pool. When he failed to change his demeanor, even after being warned by the grenade, a 2½ ton truck accidentally lost its parking brakes and slid down onto his bunker. The bunker was damaged, but he wasn't.

"Aim going to get that godaaam sonomabitch that truck was assigned to and kick his godaaaam aaass."

He was screaming all over the compound. The next day, the XO, Sheridan, called Pyatte over.

"Listen Sarge, don't you think that it's a little strange that you found a live grenade in your bunker? Then you're nearly killed by a 2½ ton truck? I hate to tell you this, but you better lay off of the men, or someone is going to fragg you."

Pyatte said, "I'll be goddaam. I'm gonna find out who is doing this."

"Look Pyatte", said the XO, "you don't seem to understand. They're going to kill you if you don't let up, and there's nothing I can do about it unless I find out who they are, do you understand?"

"Shit", said Pyatte, then I'm going to get the hell out of here. You have to transfer me out sir."

Look, Pyatte, I can't transfer you out of here, so you better get smart real quick."

The next day one of the guys heard Pyatte on a trans-Atlantic phone call.

"Honey, I don't care what you goddaam have to do, but go down to the Red Cross, and tell them I'm needed back home. These crazy sumabitches are going to kill me if I don't get out of here!"

Several days later a call came through from the Red Cross asking the Battery Commander to authorize a month's emergency leave because his wife was sick.

As time went on, my mind and body began adjusting to the climate and the war. The year, 1967 was swiftly coming to an end. Christmas was approaching, but it didn't have the familiar feel of the Christmas seasons I had known. We placed Christmas decorations everywhere, and the Chaplain tried to set the mood, as was expected of him. He tried in vain to keep up the morale of the men. This Christmas had the feeling of hopelessness to him and too many of the men.

Vietnam was a terribly boring place when we weren't flying. The evenings were so insufferably long, that some nights we hoped to be rocketed just for something to do. Drinking for many of us broke the monotony. We not only drank at night, and whenever we were not scheduled to fly, but some of the guys turned to smoking pot. Hell, the stuff grew wild behind the tents. None of our guys were real drug abusers, although I understand that back home the 'television-war' showed many men were on drugs. But I can say without hesitation that the Div-arty guys were not like that. We all tried pot every now and then, but nobody was really into it. I personally didn't care for it, so I stuck to my beer drinking like most.

One evening one of the guys brought over a movie, projector, and screen. When it was set up, we all took a comfortable seat so we could see whatever it was we were given to watch. We didn't know the title because the film had been passed around so much that it wore the name off the metal container. The movie started with two women walking into an apartment that belonged to a gay male friend. They proceeded to take off his clothes with a subtitle saying, "We'll change him back to loving woman when we're through with him". It was my first pornographic movie experience. I was a little shocked. I'd heard about these movies, but had never seen one. For most of the guys it was hot. The steam was pouring off of our backs. Someone said, "Quick, I need a bucket of ice water". Another first experience for me courtesy of Uncle Sam.

Most flight missions required us to fly visual reconnaissance. The night radar would monitor enemy troop movements. We would receive a mission sheet directing us to the suspected area. On occasion, our helicopters would be supported by two Navy jets from the aircraft carrier Coral Sea. If we made a sighting, we would drop a smoke marker. Then the jets would come in and napalm the area. Later we would return after the fire was out, and try to get a body count.

Spotting for artillery was different. We would do what is called "flying the arch". That meant that we would be flying back and forth under the arch of the artillery projectile. That allowed us to direct the shelling more accurately to correspond with enemy movement.

Lieutenant Mullins, the Operations Officer, came by to talk to me about moving north with him.

"Russo, they're setting up a new base of operations up north. I'm dying to get out of this job as Operations Officer. I need to get in more flying time. I could use someone with your experience. Would like you to join me? What do you say?"

"Well LT, life is beginning to get a little boring here. What the hell, let's go. Why don't we take that hillbilly bastard Billy Ray with us? He's a pretty good crew chief."

I received verbal orders to pack up, and head North to help set up a new base camp. I was told it would be known as Camp Eagle. I for one, was happy to move. The war was too slow for my blood. Let's get into it, I thought. This is beginning to get very boring. Unfortunately, I didn't listen to my old pappy when he said, "be very careful of what you wish for, because it might come true."

I remember now how crazy or maybe just plain stupid we were. Bob and Zok had their eyes on a couple of women in the next village. They had borrowed a couple of Vesper motor scooters, two 45 cal. hand guns, two passes, and decided to slip into town to find the ladies. Although they were wearing civilian clothes, they weren't fooling anyone. Their whole appearance shouted military. It happened to be one of the darkest nights of the year. The perimeter gates were closed, and nobody was allowed in or out without the proper pass.

As the two drove into the village they began to realize that the 'witching hour' was approaching. The VC came out of hiding late at night, and reaped havoc with the troops.

Stopping at an unlit intersection, they noticed shadows. Bob turned to Zok.

"Let's get the fuck out of here. I don't want to get laid that bad. I don't like the looks of this at all."

Zok said, "Bob, we're only a couple of clicks from their huts. Let's go for it."

It was just about that time a little window across an alley opened, and they saw the blasts aimed directly at them. They fled back to camp as fast as they could go. As they were driving through the dirt roads, Bob said a little prayer.

"God, if I get back alive, I will go to church every Sunday without fail."

At one point he noticed tracers following him down the road. The Vespers were wide open, and the wind was burning their eyes and making them water. Again he said another prayer.

"Lord if I get back from this trip, I will give $10.00 to the poor in Hue for as long as I am here."

As they turned the corner he could see the gates to the camp and reconsidered.

"Well lord, maybe $10.00 as long as I am here is a little too much, and going to services every week may be very hard to do. Lord, you know how it is in the military, life is tough, I guess I'll try to go as often as I can, but thanks for letting us return alive. Amen."

Arriving at the bunker, both laughed....phew, that was fucking close.

Zok "I need a joint. I gotta have a smoke. Bob you want some smoke?"

"No way Zok. You know I hate that shit....give me some panther piss, and a lot of it. I'm never going to let you talk me into doing something that stupid again. We're fuck'n crazy."

We did do a lot stupid, crazy, juvenile things to keep from getting bored. One evening, to break the monotony, we decided to sneak up to a couple of high ranking officers' tents, and tie smoke grenades with tripwire to the entrance of the tents. The lines were attached directly in front of the tent's entrance as well as to both sides. As one of the Majors' was exiting his tent to take a shower, I heard a popping of the grenade. The next thing I heard was the Major screaming at the top of his lungs.

"I'll get you, you fucking Russo. I know you did this. You and fucking Peterson and Bader. You've all had it."

We couldn't see him because the smoke from the grenade was very thick; it had covered half of the camp. I don't think I ever laughed so hard, especially when he started to scream out our names. I don't know why he automatically assumed it was us, but that was OK. He knew it was just fun. I think after that night he slept with one eye opened. He just didn't trust us...with good reason!

A few days later the Major had his chance to get back at me. After returning from a flight, I noticed a couple of the guys trying to light a barrel full of trash on fire. I should have known that this was a setup when one of the guys motioned for me to come over to help.

"You guys are too stupid to even light a drum full of trash. What shit heads! Give me those matches."

In Vietnam, we burned everything, but little did I know that the Major had them pour gasoline into the barrel, and it had settled in the bottom? The barrel had holes punched into the bottom, so naturally I decided to light the trash from the bottom! It only makes sense; the flame would rise to the top and ignite.

As I placed the match near the hole, the barrel exploded, and the trash went flying into the air. One of the guys yelled "incoming" and started running. I did the same. As I ran up the hill toward the bunkers, the trash from the barrel started to fall hitting me on the head. I can remember one soda can hitting me squarely on top of my head. By the time I realized what had happened, half of the unit was standing around the bunkers laughing, clapping and whistling. The Major stepped out of the crowd, smiled, bent over tipping his hat, bowing to all. He turned to me, and pointing his finger yelled, "Payback's a Bitch!"

During our earlier days in-country, since we were on flight status, we were not yet totally aware of the harsh realities of the war. Unlike a lot of other soldiers, we didn't have to break our backs carrying everything needed to survive through the jungles. We weren't scared half out of our wits all of the time, yet. We didn't have to contend with jungle rot or mildewed boots, and we didn't have to sleep in the wet humid jungle in our ponchos. The Vietnam War still seemed distant considering we were in the heart of it. The days were long and hot and the nights were very, very lonely.

It was one of those long hot days, when my aircraft was taken off flight status for scheduled maintenance that Zok and I drove into the Marine Seabee base for materials we needed to make some furniture. The Seabees were the engineering part of the Marines. They had everything we needed to build anything. We figured, we could do some trading. We had some Russian AK rifles that we could use for trade.

The AK's were picked up after finding a cache in one of the LZ's. On the way there, we passed the Seabee's bar, so we decided to stop in for a cool one. After all, they had iced cold beer. Sure, we had beer, but it was rarely cold. What we really needed was a good refrigerator. After downing two brews, we were told that they were out of beer until the evening ration was available, whatever that meant.

While leaving the building, it struck me. Right in front of my eyes was the answer to our problem. There was a chain link fence protecting a yard full of refrigerators. All we had to do was talk these CB's out of one little unit. That shouldn't be a problem, right? Wrong! That night we returned to the bar and found the NCO in charge of the refrigerators. The NCO had a real deep voice.

"Now you boys want one of my beautiful coolers, eh?"

Zok said, "Just tell us what you'll take in trade, and we'll get it for you."

As they were talking, I noticed a crew chief from the First Cavalry wearing a winter flight jacket. I wanted that jacket. You see everyone had summer flight jackets, but when the monsoon season came we would freeze our butts off. I wanted that jacket. So, I strolled up to the crew chief.

"Hey buddy, great flight jacket. How can you stand the heat with that thing on?"

"Well" he replied, "I stand it just fine."

I asked, "how about making a little trade. I'll give you a brand new summer flight jacket for it."

He scratched his head a little and said, "nah, I don't need a summer jacket."

I said, "Tell me what you want."

He was a little irritated, "I don't want anything, just leave me alone."

About this time Zok came over to me shaking his head.

"He won't deal. I knew he wouldn't."

Since we weren't having much luck with our negotiations, Zok and I settled down for a few beers. This time we decided to order at least six beers at once. The bartender thought we were with the bunch of guys in the corner of the room, so he gave us that many. We figured when they ran out of beer, we would have enough to keep us busy for a while.

The night continued on, and we continued to drink. The only problem was, the club never ran out of beer. So we had at least six beers each when we realized that they weren't going to run out of beer that night. With six beers on the table, added to the several we had as we checked out the place, we were so drunk we could hardly find our way to the truck. To make matters worse, on the way out the door, the crew chief grabbed my arm.

"I'll tell you what. I'll trade the flight jacket for a hand gun. Can you get me one?"

I told him, "No problem."

He continued, "The only problem is, that if I don't get it tonight, the deal doesn't happen. I'm moving up North tomorrow morning."

This was unbelievable!

I said, "What! I have to go back 15 miles to get you that gun, and find my way back here in the dark?"

As it was, I was holding onto the truck for fear of falling, and I was having difficulty getting my upper lip to meet my bottom lip to form words. I looked at Zok who was not in much better shape. We were smashed, drunk out of our minds.

Zok said, "We can do it Russky. I know this place like the *plaque* of my hand."

He couldn't talk straight.

I said, "I hope you know the way, because I'm too drunk to see."

It was a long way back. We traveled for what seemed to be hours. We bounced around, in and out of holes and bomb craters. At one point Zok asked me, "Is that the road?"

I answered, "Looks like a road to me, Zok. Let's try it!"

We drove right into a bomb crater. We both bounced off the windshield.

Zok shouted, "Now look, we broke the windshield. How am I going to explain that?"

"Don't worry," I said, "I'll take care of everything after I get my flight jacket."

Believe it or not, we made it back despite our drunkenness, the darkness, and the craters. It seemed as though we always made it one way or another. I think it was just sheer luck that we didn't kill ourselves without help from the enemy. I gave him my issued 38 Special, and he gave me his winter flight jacket. It was probably the only one in country. I was happy with the deal. Actually, almost anything would make us happy back then. I still had that flight jacket until a few years ago when I decided to send the jacket to one of Zok's sons in Oregon.

The next day I explained to the guys.

"I have an idea how we can get a refrigerator from the Seabee's. Zok, you get some straps strong enough to lift and carry a fridge. Someone can take the straps, climb the fence and strap up the unit. At that point we'll come in with a huey, hook on the fridge, and pull it out to its new home."

Everyone was silent, probably awed by the sheer brilliance of the plan.

"Don't think about it too long because it might start to make sense to you dopes."

"Let's do it" Pete said, "I don't know who'll climb the fence, and what about the aircraft markings?"

Then Pete remembered, "Hey, I'm coming back from a mission in Cambodia tomorrow. All of the letters will be covered by tape. That's the best time to do it, when all of the ID markings are covered. We'll do it in broad daylight. There are so many hueys flying around they'll think it's just a plane flying a little too close to the ground."

We all agreed that tomorrow was to be the day. When Pete flew the mission to Cambodia, he had to tape over the numbers of the aircraft, and any US Army insignias because we weren't supposed to be in that country's airspace. Like they didn't know who we were. The Ho Chi Minh trail ran all along the border between Cambodia and Vietnam. When flying the trail, we were looking for large concentrations of men and equipment on the move. That would give intelligence a pretty good idea where the enemy may infiltrate that night. It was so easy it was almost a joke.

Before Pete left on his mission, he borrowed a mobile radio. He made up some story about needing to check his radio frequencies. Zok also took a radio, and that afternoon waited by the Seabee Club for Pete to call. As the saying goes, "if we didn't have bad luck, we'd have no luck at all." So as luck would have it, when it was time to call the aircraft, the radio didn't work. They were forced to buzz the area several times. Zok quickly climbed the fence, picked out a fridge and started tying it up. I was outside of the fence. I guess I was supposed to be the lookout. I noticed Zok was having a hard time placing the straps around the fridge. Then I realized why he was having such a hard time of it. He was laughing so hard that he couldn't get the job done. I guess I was supposed to be the lookout. I was pacing, nervous as a cat because this was not exactly going as planned.

It was hot, and as the aircraft approached, it was blowing sand everywhere. Finally, the straps were on, and we signaled for the pickup. They came in nice and slow. As the aircraft hovered over the refrigerator, something happened that we didn't count on. The down wash from the helicopter blades started to lift and rip the roof shingles off the Club. The men inside came out of the Club to see what was going on. When they saw Zok, they started screaming.

One of them said, "Get out of here you son-of-a-bitch. I'll kill you if I get hold of you!"

Zok couldn't hear him because of the engine and prop noise, but I think he got the drift. When the refrigerator was hooked on, he motioned to the huey to go. However, he wasn't taking any chances with the Seabee's, so he grabbed hold of the straps, and flew out with the fridge. I watched them go down the road and out of sight. There was roofing material everywhere. The NCO in charge came over to me.

He said, "What do you know about this? I know you're in on it."

"What are you talking about, I said, I thought the plane was in trouble, so I stopped to help."

He gave me a look...if looks could kill...I started my vehicle and drove off.

A while later I still had a hard time hearing from standing so close to all the noise of the aircraft without benefit of protection. Sand was in my hair and all over my clothes. It was a damn good thing the numbers of that helicopter were covered, because we'd probably have landed in the brig for sure. When they returned to base camp with the refrigerator, nobody even questioned where it came from. They just plugged it in and stocked it full of beer.

CHAPTER 12

We arrived at what was to be our new base camp, Camp Eagle, around Christmas. Vietnam did not provide a cheery backdrop for the holiday. I remember that most of the guys were looking forward to the cease-fire TET plans between the North and the South. For several thousand years, the Vietnamese lunar New Year had been a celebration that the Vietnamese believed brought them happiness, hope and peace. We were beginning to relax and unwind because the Vietnamese had negotiated a cease-fire. Christmas was fine and we almost had the whole day off as we tried to forget the war.

After relaxing for several days, we were suddenly jolted by the TET Offensive. It was one of the worst combat actions against our forces while in country. There were hundreds; some say thousands of Vietcong and North Vietnamese regulars trying to come through the wires. Rockets came in from everywhere. It was said that while planning the 1968 offensive, the North Vietnamese Army had imitated the strategy of one of their great heroes, King Quong Trung, who won a great victory over his Chinese aggressors in a 1789 counter attack.

The offensive started on TET's eve in the early morning of January 30th. 1968. The city of Hue, Phu Bai, Camp Eagle and Danang were hit from the communist 5th military region. The southern cities were hit 24 hours later... January 31st included Saigon. This large-scale offensive resulted in a large loss of communist forces. It also resulted in increased protests, further turning American public opinion against the war. There were many exaggerations and outright lies told not only about the Offensive, but what was happening in Vietnam period. From what we heard, it seemed the American public was continuously and purposefully misinformed about that War.

It was about 3:00 A.M. when the first set of rockets started to drop. Mortars, and what I thought was small arms fire, accompanied the rockets. I grabbed my helmet, threw on my boots, and ran to the bunker with the other guys. We never wore underwear because of the heat. Try to picture us sitting in the bunkers just wearing helmets and boots and nothing else. The rockets had that distinctive crackling sound as they came overhead. They were coming closer and closer to our bunker. The bombing lasted for only a few minutes, but those minutes seemed like hours. Then, just as fast as it started, it stopped. I swear I could hear everyone's heart pounding, including my own. We were hardly breathing when Barrera, whispered.

"I hear voices...shush," everyone was quiet. "They're gook voices."

None of us had taken weapons with us to the bunkers.

Barrera, "I'll slip back and get some weapons, don't make a sound."

Make a sound, we were barely breathing. I could hear Barrera moving things around looking for his weapon in the dark. He returned shortly bringing with him a 38 and an M-16. It was just about then we started to hear popping noises about 150 yards from us. It was mortar tubes popping off inside the compound.

Barrera, "The gooks are in the compound shooting off mortars. We need to knock them out."

He passed the M-16 to Bill Bader, "Let's go Bill. It's time to earn our pay."

They slipped out of the bunker and into the darkness. In the meantime, Zok and I decided to try and get our weapons. I crawled into the tent, scraping my knees, elbows and a few other body parts. It could have been worse. I could have damaged the family jewels. I threw on some pants and my flack jacket, grabbed any weapon I could find, and then I dove back to the bunker for cover. By this time we were all pretty well pumped up. As soon as I settled back into the bunker, I heard Bill and Barrera exchanging small arms fire with the insurgents down by the wire.

Fifteen minutes later the guns were silenced, and I heard the men coming back up the hill.

"It's us, don't shoot."

They were running, and with one big dive jumped into the bunker. They were both out of breath and sweating. You could tell just by looking at them that their adrenaline was pumping. They looked like wild men. They were talking so fast, that we couldn't understand what they were saying.

"Guys, calm down. Talk so we can understand you."

Barrera started, "There were three gooks. They had a mortar pod set up, and were firing mortars from inside the compound. We would never have found them."

Then Bill interrupted, "I shot at least ten rounds in their direction, hoping to hit at least one of them. It was too dark to tell if we got them until we rushed their position. They're dead."

I asked, "Are you sure they're dead?"

Barrera said, "I made sure they were dead with a couple more rounds."

After Bill and Barrera calmed down, I could see the blank expressions on their faces. Bill was the first to speak.

"I never killed anyone before. I hope I don't have to go down there and bring up their bodies."

Barrera, "I've seen bodies from the air, but never this close before, especially killing someone that close."

The both of them felt the remorse we all feel after our first kill. I guess we wouldn't be human if killing didn't bother us. The rockets and mortars started to hit our position again, and they continued to pound our location throughout the night. It was one of the longest nights I could remember.

The next morning the word was out all across the country. The North Vietnamese staged an all-out offensive. This happened during a time when the North was believed to be incapable of performing such a feat.

Vietnamese bodies were everywhere. Front-end loaders had to plow them into mass graves. The large majority of the bodies were in the wires, caught as they tried to come over into the compound. This happened in Saigon, Bien Hoi, and at most of the outposts around the country. This offensive surprised both politicians back in Washington and high-ranking military officers alike. This action seemed so inconceivable because the North, who was thought to have depleted their strength, almost pulled off a miracle. After the offensive, we received mortar attacks on a nightly basis along with more frequent ground action.

As I strolled past the Battery Commander's tent, I noticed a huge mortar crater in the ground. It couldn't have been more than six feet from the entrance to his tent.

Captain Goodbolt, "Hey, Russo, what do you think about their aim?"

"Pretty good for night firing, sir!"

Goodbolt, "They were excellent artillerymen. It's too bad we had to kill them."

The Commander, "Russo, come in and get debriefed. After we're done, I have a little mission for you."

When debriefing was completed, the Commander directed us to pick up a Battalion Commander located at Phu Bai Airport. When we flew into Phu Bai to pick him up, we could see that the Commander had his artillery battalion disbursed throughout the area. The Phu Bai Airport was predominately operated by the Air Force with a section operated by Marine aviation units on the opposite side of the field.

One big problem with the Vietnam War was that the various military branches frequently worked independently of each other, and when they did work together they didn't appear to work as a team. They were, at times, uncooperative with each other. Hard to imagine that we were all there for the same reason yet there was still competition among the different branches. Our branch, Army aviation, was given a hard time every time we had to refuel at a non-Army airport. The conversations between the tower and the aircraft were sometimes very hostile.

"Phu Bai Airport, this is Eagle Gunner seven-niner-six, five miles south your location and landing, over."

"This is Phu Bai tower, seven-niner-six. What is your intention, over."

"Phu Bai Tower, we intend to land and pick up passengers at the north side of the field, over."

"Eagle gunner seven-niner-six, be advised that your aircraft will not be allowed to refuel unless you have advance approval from command, over."

This antagonistic type of conversation between military branches was too common. I think someone forgot to tell them that we were on the same side, fighting the same war.

That morning, as we were approaching the airfield, the tower also notified us that they were under mortar attack. Unfortunately, we didn't believe them because of the fuel situation, and we had no intention of letting them get the best of us.

"Are they shitting me or what? They're getting ridiculous with this shit. Now they're getting spiteful on top of being assholes. Fuck them, we're going in, mortars my ass."

We were descending from the south side of the field. As we approached, we could see the artillery vehicles lined up at the opposite end. When we descended to about fifty feet, all hell broke loose. Mortar and artillery fire erupted all around the airfield. The rounds exploded like fireworks shooting off in all directions. I thought I heard flak hit the tail of the aircraft.

"Zok, can you see if the tail was hit?"

Zok's intercom was breaking up. None of us could hear him. A quick decision had to be made; land or take a chance of flying out in heavy flak with a damaged aircraft. The decision was to land. It just wasn't safe to be flying through a barrage of ordinance with a bad tail rotor.

The tower hadn't been lying. The action around the airfield was very heavy. Of course the airfield had to close. We took unnecessary chances because of the mistrust between the different branches of the military. The whole thing was stupid.

Once we were on the ground we moved quickly, with the rotor blades still turning we headed for the closest bunker. After a couple of hours of being pounded by artillery and rockets, it stopped. Zok and Pete went to evaluate the damage to the craft, while I went to see the Battalion Commander. I found him in what was left of the Mess Tent.

He said, "Grab a tray, and get some chow while you can. I want to pick a location for my men to set up before night fall."

I said, "I don't think so, sir."

"What! Perhaps you didn't hear me."

"Yes, sir, I heard you."

"Then what's the problem?"

"The problem is twofold, sir. The first problem is the aircraft. We sustained damages. The men are checking the aircraft now. The second problem is the weather. Fog will have us closed in before night fall."

"Well, I want to be out of here before it gets dark, keep me informed!"

"Yes, sir. I will."

I took a mess tray and headed for the serving line. The cook placed some sort of mystery meat on the tray.

"Hey! What the hell is this?"

The cook just smiled. I gave him my meanest look, but it didn't have any affect. I think he'd seen that same look before.

He said, "This is canned hot dogs" (he sounded like a redneck). There were a lot of rednecks in the military.

"That's all we have until the food supplies arrive, and they won't arrive until the field reopens."

That's military life for you! They run you ragged, and what do they give you....*canned* hot dogs!

Then, of course, to make life even more miserable it started to rain heavily. The rain wasn't like we have back home. It was monsoon season, and the rain was heavier than you could ever imagine. Shit, what else can go wrong? I didn't have to wait long to find out. In a couple of minutes Zok and Pete returned from checking the aircraft just as the rain was at its worst. Pete, who was trying to shake off the rain, came over to me.

Pete, "Bad news. The radio received a couple of rounds, and the tail rotor received shrapnel. We probably lucked out when we decided to land."

"Why don't you guys get some chow? After we eat, we'll call back to base camp to see if they could send us replacement parts and radios."

After an hour of monsoon rain pelting us, it slowly changed to mist and then heavy fog. The airport and surrounding area was socked in. It was all so quiet, and as fog began to roll in, it became downright eerie. We could barely see the vehicles. The wind stopped blowing, and when someone spoke, it echoed for what seemed like miles. I didn't like it at all.

Zok called back to the maintenance tent for replacement radios and a tail rotor.

Lt. Baker answered, "Dubin, tell Russo that the heavy fog and rain has all aircraft grounded. Also, the reports we're receiving say that there are North Vietnamese regulars all over your location. With this rain and fog, nobody can get to you guys. You better hope that this clears up fast because otherwise those NVA will knock the shit out of your position and the airfield. As soon as it clears up, we'll send you the equipment. Until then, keep your heads down and try to stay dry."

As Zok turned to relay the message, we heard that now familiar crackling sound from overhead again. The voices rang out, "incoming". I looked out of the tent to see a pattern of explosions headed in our direction. It was a full barrage of mortar fire. We dropped our trays and headed for bunkers, bomb craters, or any other hole we could find or crawl into.

The attack on the airfield was heavy and long. I remember looking out of a bomb crater and seeing mud and dirt filling the air around us. I don't mind telling you that I was scared shitless. I could tell that everyone around me felt the same. All I had to do was look at their faces. Fear was written all over them. A big dark shadow of a man ran by me. He was so close that I felt the wind as he passed. In front of him was a Major who had just slipped and fallen. The soldier literally walked right over the Major stepping right on his back as he dove into a bunker. The sight was so funny that I couldn't stop laughing. I almost couldn't catch my breath, I was laughing so hard. It was really funny to see the expression on the Major's face.

After the Major got up and jumped in the bunker he grabbed the soldier.

"Do you know who I am soldier? You stepped on top of me! What do you have to say for yourself?"

The soldier was soaked with a mix of perspiration and rain.

"Sorry sir, I was scared, that's all, just scared."

With that, the soldier cracked a little smile. Luckily the Major was very understanding and could take a joke.

"Well, at least clean your boot prints off my back before you sit down."

I could hear everyone within earshot laughing, and so could the Major.

The hours of being stranded at the airfield grew into days. We were at that airport without a change of clothes, and the only thing to eat was canned hot dogs. Hot dogs for breakfast, lunch and dinner. Hot dogs...hot dogs....hot dogs!

Billy Rae Sextant was one of our flight crewmembers. Billy Rae was from the Ozark Mountains, a good old boy who mostly kept to himself. After a few days of eating canned hotdogs, he came over and told me that he had seen an old farmhouse with a chicken coop just outside the perimeter. He suggested that we go to the farm house that night and pick us up a couple of chickens for breakfast. I thought it was a great idea. Anything was better than canned hot dogs.

That evening we slipped out through the perimeter and found the path that led to the chicken coop. The overcast skies made it pitch black, and nearly impossible to find our way. We did, however, finally locate the coops, but couldn't see what we were doing.

The night air was cool, still and very quiet until I opened the door, reached in and grabbed a handful of feathers. At that very instant the chickens started clucking and squawking. I took my chicken, and placed him in a sack. Billy Rae did the same. However, we weren't quite finished. I thought it was a little too easy, and I was right. As we began to make our way back, small arms fire started to go off near the tree line.

I called to Billy Rae, "What the fuck is that? Let's get the fuck out of here. It's that fuck'n farmer shooting at us."

Billy Rae crawled over beside me. "I don't think it's the farmer shooting at us. That sounds like AK 47's."

Bad news for us because we didn't take any weapons with us. We had nothing with us to defend ourselves except a couple of chickens. Then we heard yelling in Vietnamese. Suddenly all was quiet, then in English we heard.

"I see you paratroopers. I shoot you and take chickens, paratroop. You come, give chickens, and we no shoot."

Billy Rae whispered to me, "Fuck him, he's no farmer, and I'll bet there's a bunch of them."

As the next volley of small arms rang out, Billy Ray said, "Did you hear all of that? There must be at least five of them."

It was a good thing that it was so dark. The bullets were whizzing over our heads as we ate dirt, and crawled as fast as we could. Slowly the sound started to fade. Just when we thought we were safe, we heard shooting again. This time the shots were in front of us.

"Shit", we're surrounded."

My mind went blank. I didn't have the slightest idea what we were going to do. Again, we started to hear voices, and they were beginning to get closer as we continued to crawl. I could hear that the voices were in English, and realized that they were American. I thought, now our own men are attacking us. Apparently, in all of the confusion, we went in the wrong direction, and ended up near a perimeter guard post.

I yelled, "Hey you guys, don't shoot, we're Americans."

A voice yelled back, "What's the password?"

Billy Rae yelled, "I don't know, but don't shoot."

The perimeter guard yelled, "I'm going to light a flare, stand up with your hands on your head."

I yelled, "We can't, we have some gooks behind us trying to shoot our asses."

Just then two flares were popped, and the area lit up like daylight. Firing started from behind us shooting at the perimeter post. The guard post started to return the fire with us caught between them. All I can remember is eating a lot of dirt. The firefight probably lasted only about a minute, but when the guns are aimed at you, a minute was much too long.

Then I felt my arm pop into the air as several bullets passed by. It was a strange feeling. I didn't feel any pain, but blood was running down my arm. How could that be? Perhaps my arm was so numb that I couldn't feel the pain.

The perimeter guards directed us to crawl over a ravine and away from the minefield, and then told us to slide into camp. As we entered their field of sight, one of the men started to yell at us.

"You two stupid fucks should be dead now. You must have luck up your asses.

I could tell that the guard was all hyped up. That usually happens following intense action. As we were passing the guards, I remember telling Billy Rae that I wouldn't mind eating hot dogs for breakfast anymore.

Dropping into the guard's bunker the light from a small flashlight was enough for us to see the surroundings and the blood all over me. Billy Rae grabbed my shirt.

"You've been hit! There's blood all over your arm."

I started to feel around my arm and chest, nothing, no pain. I passed the bag of chickens to him.

"Here, hold this."

As he was taking the bag from my hand, I felt something warm dripping down my arm. It finally dawned on me. The chicken was the one shot, not me. It was *chicken* blood that I had all over me. What a relief! I thought I was in big trouble.

The next morning we gave the chickens to the cooks with our orders.

"You can make soup for the guys if you like, but I want some fried chicken for lunch."

I couldn't wait, no hot dogs for me. I practically ran to the mess tent at lunchtime.

"Hey, Spoon, is my chicken ready?"

"Billy Rae's is ready, but not yours."

I couldn't understand. I was pissed. So, I ate some of Billy Rae's, promising him that I would share my dinner when it was done. At supper the chicken still wasn't ready. I was beginning to smell a rat. I thought somebody had already eaten my chicken. I strolled around the back of the mess tent and grabbed the cook by the collar.

"Did you guys eat my chicken?"

The cook was startled.

"No, sir."

"Well then, where the fuck is it?"

He took a deep breath and said, "Well, you see, that chicken you had was an old hen. I had to boil it for seven hours to make it tender enough to fry."

The truth was Billy Rae, coming from farm country, knew enough to grab a young tender bird. What the hell did I know about chickens! So I was left holding the old bag as usual.

Finally after twenty-eight days of rain, fog and rockets our radios arrived along with enough parts to get us airborne once again. The North Vietnamese Army was forced back out of the area and the sun came out. It was great to be back at Camp Eagle again.

Getting back to the guys, one of the guys that played with us was Bob Evers Bob Evers came from Brooklyn, New York, and was very energetic in every undertaking. We all got along so well that he referred to us as a little clique or "our group". Our group had a lot of clout, so to speak. Bob was the Battery Commander's driver, and we knew the XO, who later became the Battery Commander, real well. The Battery Clerk and the Armorer were also under our influence. What else did we need? We did whatever we wanted, and received little or no opposition. In Vietnam, we were more like the characters from the TV program, MASH.

I digress. Getting back to Bob. Physically Bob was a very large imposing person. He was also loud, stubborn, and if he wanted something, it was best not to get in his way. He was what most people would consider *All American*. No drugs, clean cut, hated hippies. Although he once commented on how he thought Zok was really a hippie, but he admired him because he was a good soldier, and in his opinion, Zok did his job well.

I remember a story about Bob. It was how Bob handled a problem with two hippies while he was on leave. It seemed that these two hippies were heckling him. Bob was in uniform, and the hippies were goading him by calling him "baby killer" and "war monger". It apparently went on and on.... When Bob finally had enough he walked up to one, and slapped him with a backhand so hard that he was knocked to the ground. Then Bob grabbed the second hippie and pulled him into an alley. I did say Bob was a big boy....get the drift? Bob grabbed him by the throat with one hand, and by the hair with the other. He then commenced ripping out the hippie's hair. There was blood and hair everywhere. The on-lookers were applauding and the hippie was screaming. I was told it was quite a scene.

Being so very far north created problems, like a shortage of electricity to show movies, run refrigerators or lights so we could just drink and play cards. Bob had decided that we weren't going to continue living like this anymore, so he grabbed a jeep, asked me and Zok to take a ride to the Seabee base.

He told Zok to drive, and as we were headed down the road Bob started to change his shirt. He decided that he was going to be a Major today. That was what he was wearing on his shirt, Major insignias. Impersonating an officer is a court martial offence, and he knew it.

I said, "OK, what kind of shit are you up to?"

"Listen", he said, "we need a small generator. Let's see if we can talk those CBs out of one."

I said, "Are you crazy? In broad daylight...Do you think they're just going to give us a generator after that refrigerator deal?"

"You can never tell, maybe they'll give us a nice little unit."

As we made our way onto the CB base, we spotted a motor pool with several different sized generators along with a guard at the entrance.

"Zok, just pull up to the guard and stopped."

As we stopped, the guard saluted Bob. Bob jumped out of the jeep with a clip board in one hand.

Pointing to his clipboard Bob said, "Private, I'm here to pick up a generator."

The Private, "Yes sir, which one is it, sir?"

Bob said, "Let me see. I think it's that one over there", pointing to a generator so large that it sat on its own trailer, and the jeep we were driving would never be able to pull it.

"Sir, I don't think that your jeep can pull that generator. You'll probably need a truck."

Bob said, "Good thinking son. We'll go back and return with a 2-1/2 ton truck. You know son, you're one hell of a guard. What is your name? I'm going to notify your commanding officer, and tell him just how much help you've been."

The private smiled, "Thank you, sir."

Bob, "Zok, hurry up. Let's get back and grab a truck before things get stupid."

This took place during the lunch hour. Therefore, we wanted to return and get that generator before lunch was over. Bob was screaming and we were laughing all the way back to camp

When we returned to our camp with the generator, we realized that the unit was so large that it would run the entire camp. The motor pool Sergeant was trying to figure out where he was going to get all the diesel fuel they needed to run that monster.

Bob, "Hey, Sergeant Brown, don't get too close, the paint is still wet."

Sgt Brown, "You fuck'n guys are always doing something. Where the hell am I going to get papers for this thing?"

"Don't worry", Bob said, "if you need papers, we'll get you some."

Brown just laugh and walked away shaking his head.

"Shit", here comes Captain Sheridan.

"Hi men. "What a great looking generator! I didn't think we could get one this large as an airborne unit. How are we supposed to get that thing on an aircraft?"

"Well sir", Bob said, "someone must have screwed up because here it is."

"Hey, he yelled, "Sergeant Brown, show the Captain the paperwork on this thing

That did it for me. I couldn't hold it in any longer. I was laughing so hard I almost wet my pants.

"OK" said Sheridan, "let's start this thing up. Good work men. See you later."

Sheridan v funny. He was over us, yet he could be c of us. He never made us feel less than him, so we genuinely liked and respected him.

CHAPTER 13

Billy Rae, Lt. (Moon) Mullins, and I received orders to fly further north and link up with the 321st Artillery to fly support at a Landing Zone named Jane. Flying support had many meanings. We could be moving troops, directing artillery from the air, delivering food or just dropping off beer and coke to guys stuck out in the bush.

Landing Zone Jane was primarily a support point for artillery. It was just a small hill in the middle of what looked like no-man's-land. From the air LZ Jane looked like a large brown circle surrounded by craters carved out by all of the bombing.

As we made our approach, dust could be seen from other helicopters landing and taking off. The perimeter was like most, surrounded with barbed wire, land mines, and anything else that they could think of to stop intruders. This was Charlie's country, and don't think he didn't take every opportunity to let us know it.

Charlie was slang for Vietcong (VC) and short for Victor Charlie. Several times a night they would send us rockets or mortars just to remind us they were out there; not so subtle reminders that we were on their turf.

After arriving at LZ Jane, we flew constantly. It was obvious that everyone loved to fly. As pilots we were in demand. Everyone needed something that was someplace else. We enjoyed keeping busy because the time would go by that much faster. When we were forced to be on the ground, we were bored to death. The only time we didn't fly was when we had bad weather.

It was just one of those nights, when the weather was bad that we received a request to take a Battery Commander back to his men. We had light rain mixed with fog, and that gave the night a particularly ominous feel. Flying was completely out of the question, or so I thought.

"No, it's below standards. Why take the chance of flying in this shit? Wait until tomorrow and see if it clears."

"Wait until tomorrow...?"

The Battery Commander expected or wanted to be with his men that night. Mullins, who was the Officer in charge, decided that he should take the flight. I tried to dissuade him.

"Lieutenant, you know that this aircraft is not rated to fly in this weather. Why are you still considering flying in it? I think I better come with you to make sure you get back so I can burn your ass with the brass."

I wanted to go along. I thought it would be safer if there were two of us, but Mullins wouldn't listen.

"There won't be enough room for you and the passengers. I'll need the extra room."

I walked out to the aircraft with him and continued to try to talk him out of the flight, but it was no use. The light rain was now a heavy mist with ground fog. It was cold and very dark. My face was wet, and the wind was making it very hard to see. Occasionally a tent flap would open and allow a little light to escape, other than that, it was raw and dark. Much too risky a night to fly.

The engine was running with the rotor blades being run up to flight rpm's. The aircraft was ready to go, and there was no stopping him. As he pulled pitch, I felt the gust of cold air in my face, and then the aircraft was immediately out of sight. Nothing to do now but wait.

I returned to my warm tent, and settled back where Billy Rae was using C-4 plastic explosive to boil some water for instant coffee.

"Billy Ray", I said, "remember what happened here tonight because when he returns, I am going to have his ass burnt. He thinks I am fucking around when I told him I was going to turn him in for taking such a chance."

The more I talked about it, the angrier I became.

"Well, I am not fucking around. He'll be lucky if he's still a lieutenant when I get done with him, the shit head. Billy Rae, don't you think he's nuts to fly tonight?"

Billy Rae just looked at me and said, "I reckon so." That was the length of the conversation. He never talked much about anything. He just went back to his chore of boiling water. Whatever he was thinking, he was keeping to himself. Some part of me both envied and admired the way Billy Rae could remain seemingly detached. He took everything in stride.

I think everyone in Vietnam used C-4 explosive for boiling water or heating food. It could make a pot of water boil almost instantly. He also designed a way to use empty howitzer shell casings filled with sand and diesel fuel to heat up the tent. Billy Ray had devised a way to cover the containers with a tent smoke stack to discharge the smoke. This kept the tent warm and dry. Billy Rae was one very resourceful guy. I guess he would have to be to survive living in the mountains.

A couple of hours went by, and I still had not heard the aircraft return. I was becoming very concerned. I figured Mullins was lost, so I decided to go out by the helipad to wait for him. After another hour my thought was to raise him by radio.

"Billy Rae, I'll bet the bastard is lost. I think I'll go out by the pad with a set of lights to see if I can guide him in."

Now, it was pouring rain, and the fog was as thick as I had ever seen it in Vietnam. I waited still another forty-five minutes, but no aircraft. Nothing. Off in the distance I could hear someone sloshing through the mud.

"Russo, is that you?"

It was the battalion's Sgt. Major.

"Russo, you'd better come down to the Command Center right away. I think you need to listen to the radio."

As I approached the Command Center, I could hear two-way radio conversations echoing back and forth. The Sgt. Major told me to go on in.

"You need to hear this."

As I entered the Command Center the radios were blasting away.

"I'm at the site now, over.

Sgt. Major, "What is the condition of the downed aircraft, over?"

The radio echoed... "The aircraft is on fire, over."

Sgt. Major, "Where is the pilot, over?"

There was a long silence. Then came the reply.

"The pilot is still in the aircraft, over."

Sgt. Major, "Can you get him out, over?"

"Negative, the aircraft is completely engulfed, over."

My heart sank with those words. I didn't want to believe it.

"Shit, Sgt. Major, ask him to repeat that last transmission?"

Sgt. Major, "You heard him right. I'll check with Division Command to find out if there was another aircraft operating in this area, but don't get your hopes up."

A few minutes later it was confirmed. It was our aircraft, and the pilot was dead. Then the guilt started to hit me. Maybe, if I was with him, I could have helped. I don't really know, but I think I was more guilt-ridden because I gave him such a hard time before he left. I also remembered that he had a wife who was pregnant.

The next morning a message was sent from the Colonel. He wanted to see me ASAP.

"You wanted to see me, sir?"

"Yes, sit down, I want you to go to the crash site and do two things. First, I want you to make sure the body isn't booby trapped so the medics can remove it. Make sure all of the parts around the body belong to the aircraft. Next, I want you to search for evidence that the aircraft was shot down. I don't want to see any pilot error or maintenance problem become the cause of this incident. I want you to report directly to me when you return to Camp. Nobody is to hear from you until I do, understand?"

I gave him a "yes, sir" and left.

We left for the crash site by truck with the doctor and medics following. The weather was drier, and the sun was trying to break through the clouds. We were slowed by some grunts walking in the road checking for land mines that may have been placed the night before. It took them several hours to walk the road with metal detectors and give the OK to pass.

As we approached the crash site we were met by some ground troops who had set up a protective perimeter while we inspected the body and the aircraft. We were now calling him a body when just ten hours ago he was a person with a name.

The ground was covered with sand, white sand. It was so white, in fact, it looked like snow. The only parts left on the aircraft intact, was the engine with part of a tail and the main rotor. Mullins' body lay directly in front of the firewall, forward of the engine. His hand was still on the control stick, and there was nothing else left to the cockpit. It didn't look like him at all. At first I had a hard time looking at the body. It looked like a burned mannequin.

Billy Rae was really the person who got right down next to the body to see if anything looked strange. He nudged me.

"Look at that. I don't remember seeing anything like that on the aircraft. What do you think?"

I looked a little closer trying not to look at the body. I noticed a small tin with a pressure release wedged under it. If we moved the body, the whole area would go up. I started to yell signaling everyone out of the area. The fuck'n plane was booby-trapped.

"Someone call for the bomb crew."

We called the experts. They came in and knew exactly what to do. The bomb was removed in a few minutes. If Billy Rae hadn't spotted that tiny little clip, we would have lost a few more men, and I would have been one of them. That's twice in 24 hours that I lucked out. How much longer would my luck hold?

The medical team examined the body on the spot. The doctor was dictating to the medic.

"He took a high powered round through the brain, neck and leg area."

He said this while placing his finger through the hole in his leg and neck. He turned to me.

"He was dead before the aircraft hit the ground, instantly."

I was relieved to know that he was not alive when the aircraft caught fire and burned. He didn't suffer. Then I noticed a piece of the flight console. It was bullet riddled. This, along with the doctor's report, gave us enough evidence to prove that it was not pilot error or a maintenance problem. As long as I live, I will still believe that he should not have flown that night.

We continued our search. We wanted to have overwhelming evidence that hostile action had in fact downed this aircraft. Billy Ray found another body part about 150 feet from the crash site. The doctor made it official after examining the part. It was a foot still inside the boot. The foot was severed by a high powered small weapons round. Then the medics placed the body in a bag, and loaded it into the truck.

After returning to the LZ, I went directly to the Colonel, and gave him my report. He was thankful that we found the cause of the accident as fast as we did. While returning to my tent, passing soldiers expressed their regrets.

The rain started again, and again it became cold, damp and dreary. That night while I was trying to sleep, visions of Mullins lying in front of what was left of the helicopter kept appearing. I heard his voice causing me to wake in a cold sweat. I needed some air. I just had to get out of that tent. Stepping out of the tent felt like a cool burst of freedom. I could breathe again. The rain on my face felt so renewing and refreshing. I can't really describe the feeling, but all I know is that I had to have that rain in my face. Just as I knew going back into the tent was out of the question. I decided to walk over to the Operations Tent. There, I knew I would be able to see and talk to live people.

The Operations Tent was dug out of the side of a hill. Most of it was an underground bunker with a tent tossed over it to keep out the rain. As I entered, the light hurt my eyes. For a few seconds I couldn't see a thing, but could feel the heat emanating from the electronic equipment in use. Someone from below yelled.

"Hey, shut that hatch before you light up the whole LZ."

I slowly made my way down to the bottom of the bunker. There I saw three men. One was a private sitting at the radio controls. Another was a Major, probably the Officer in charge. The third was the Sgt. Major. The Sgt. Major looked up.

"Oh, it's you Russo. Anything wrong? Can't you sleep?"

"No, I just needed a little air."

We were not the type of men that would admit to having a problem. We were supposed to be tough paratroopers. Nothing bothers us…right!

The Sgt. Major invited me to join him for a cup of coffee. I didn't drink coffee, but I went over anyway.

"You know", he said, "I think I was about your age when a close friend of mine was killed."

The Sgt. Major was now into his third war. He had joined the Army when he was only sixteen years old. That placed him right in the middle of WW2. He went on to fight in Korea, and now he was here in Vietnam.

He continued, "I must tell you, it was very disturbing to me, and I know that you're hurting inside. Eventually that pain will go away. I am also sure that you will never forget what you have seen, not the look on his face, or the look in his eyes. Unfortunately, you will see much more horror before you leave this place. If you ever want to talk about it, my door will always be open. You don't want to bottle it up inside. Let it go."

I listened. If anyone was an expert about the horrors of war, it would be him. I sat there trying to relax. Trying to wipe that memory out of my mind. The next thing I knew it was morning, and someone was shaking me. I must have fallen asleep at the table.

That day was much different from the previous one. The rain had stopped, and the sun was shining. I was asked to pack up the Lieutenant's personal belongings so they could be shipped home. That's the usual procedure when someone is killed in action. Later that day I was notified that another pilot and aircraft was being sent up as a replacement. War stops for no one.

The replacement pilot was a Warrant Officer named Kusterman. I can't remember his first name because we always just called him Kusterman. I wasn't really sure why Kusterman was in the military. He must have been drafted directly from college. I felt certain he was not here voluntarily. I suppose he decided to make the best of it, and go to Flight School.

He liked nothing better than to get stoned, he was a good pilot, and never smoked on the job. However, after the workday was over he would meet with some of the guys, enlisted or otherwise and get stoned. He used words like "bummer", "let's get some groceries" and "he has some good shit in his tent". He was a good ole boy with wings. He wasn't a parachutist, and had no plans to go to Jump School, but he was an OK guy. Kusterman was average height, a little chunky and usually had a smile on his face. In Vietnam that kind of attitude was 50% of the job in a Combat Zone. He flew several missions with us prior to being called back to Camp Eagle.

After permanent replacements arrived, we went back to our mission of flying artillery support. Several months went by without any substantial losses. Our nightly routine consisted of rockets and mortars every couple of hours. Our days were filled with trying to beat the heat, and counting the remaining number of days before we would return home to civilization.

One evening I was sitting out in front of our bunker with not much to do, but trying to keep cool. When all of a sudden there were incoming rockets. Every time I heard it, my heart would beat a little harder. By then we had become expert in judging their distance, by the pitch in the crackle. We watched as they began to go off about 1000 yards from us. Slowly they were making their way to our location. It was a barrage starting about 1000 yards away and slowly dropping 25 to 50 yards each time they were launched. When they seemed to be getting too close for comfort, we would head for the bunkers.

Later that evening, without warning, rockets started to go off around our tents. A rocket went off about 50 feet from me and landed by Billy Rae. He was hit, I was lucky. I then started hearing small arms fire coming from the perimeter, and the perimeter towers returned fire. Someone yelled.

"They're hitting the outer lines."

The whole LZ was in turmoil. The rockets and mortars continued to go off in the compound. NVA regulars were attacking our position. Normally we would not be encountering North Vietnamese regulars. Most of the time we were hit and run by the Vietcong. The difference between the two was the training they received in Hanoi.

The enemy was throwing hand grenades into the minefields in an attempt to clear their way into the compound. Smoke was everywhere and soldiers were running in all directions. It was getting ever so dark and becoming more difficult to see by the minute.

In between explosions I would inch my way over to Billy Rae. He needed help badly, so the last 100 feet, I got up and ran over to him. He had a piece of shrapnel about 3 inches from his right eye. He was dazed and in shock. I called for a medic, but none came. The noise was too loud for anyone to hear me. I slid myself under him and placed him on my shoulders. He was much heavier than I thought. I was having a hard time picking him up. So, I slowly started to crawl with him on my back. When I was in a position to raise myself to a full stand a mortar round landed about 30 feet from me blowing my legs out from under me. A couple of the guys witnessed what had happened and worked their way down to help.

As we entered the medics' tent, they were ready for us.

"Doc, take care of Billy Rae. I think he was hit in the eye."

The doc looked at me and then at him. We were both covered with blood. I think I was covered with his blood more than with my own. The doctor worked on him, while I was attended by one of the medics.

This doctor was a real weird person. He was constantly drunk, and I often wondered how he made it through medical school. I know he was drafted, but he probably stumbled his way through Officer's Training for Professionals. The Commander was constantly on his case about the state of his uniform or other poor military protocol. I guess we had to use whoever we had, and just make the best of it.

Billy Rae and I were both lucky. The shrapnel missed his eye and lodged in his skull. As for me, the rocket embedded part of the ground in my legs. All I needed was a few stitches, and I was back on my feet in a couple of days. As for Billy Rae, he was sent back to a Mash Unit to recuperate. They didn't even send him home. He would return to the unit when he recovered.

The NVA had penetrated the perimeter, and were very close to over running the LZ. Navy jets had to be called in to napalm the outer perimeter area. This time the Navy was a little too close for comfort. A few feet either way, and we would have been toast. Sometimes it felt like we were watching a movie, and everything that was happening, was happening to someone else. After the jets left the area, several gunships came in, and helped to clean out the rest of them. Otherwise it could have meant a complete loss of the LZ.

As the smoke and noise started to subside, I decided to go and take a look at the damage. As I limped around I saw debris everywhere. Men were helping the injured into hueys for transporting back to Mash Units. I stopped to light up a cigarette. Then I noticed that my hands were shaking uncontrollably. I still couldn't understand why this was happening to me. During the two-hour siege, I hadn't noticed the adrenaline that had compelled me and the others to keep our cool. But, now that it was over, the full impact of what we had been through hit like a ton of bricks. Although nobody mentioned it, we were all pretty scared. I could feel every muscle in my body. As I limped through the LZ, I saw one man standing over what was left of his buddy. He was crying uncontrollably. The medics were trying to talk him away, but they finally decided to just give him a few minutes to calm down.

On the backside of the LZ, I could see hueys bringing additional troops in to secure and maintain the perimeter. Once again we watched as the medics filled the black body bags. We all had the same thought; someday one of those bags might be for me.

As replacement troops continued to arrive during the following weeks, we noticed that they were different from us. They were mainly draftees. Unlike most of us Paratroopers, who volunteered for hazardous duty, these guys didn't want anything to do with the military. They had to be told three or four times to do things because they just weren't motivated. We knew that we couldn't trust them to be there for us if we needed them. Experience told me that this attitude was going to get many of them killed, and maybe take some of us with them. At night some of them would find a secluded area and smoke pot or shoot dope. When they returned home, their drug problems would be blamed on the military and their tour in Vietnam, but in truth they were druggies before they were drafted.

Don't get me wrong, we all smoked a little pot every now and then. I guess these people were a sign of the changing times in America. They were not there to fight out of pride for their country, as some of us were, and as other generations had. They were drafted and were simply marking time until they could return home. They believed everything was owed to them as a right for being born American. They didn't understand what a privilege it was to be an American.

The year was 1968 and according to the replacements from back home we were all considered baby killers and warmongers, and we didn't deserve to go home. Nobody wanted us. We were doing what we were ordered to do, as all military men have done throughout our history. Our country told us what it needed done, and we did it. We couldn't speak for ourselves through the media, because the media didn't want to hear what we had to say. Our opinions weren't considered news; besides, we were too busy fighting to bring this horrid war to a conclusion. We had to rely on others to defend us, and speak for us.

CHAPTER 14

Upon returning to Camp Eagle my CO decided that I needed to relax for a while. I couldn't have agreed more. I was sent down to China Beach for a couple of days of R & R. China Beach was a few minutes from the Danang airport. There was nothing to do but drink and watch movies. Actually, I never knew I visited China Beach until I saw the TV show with the same name many years later. I knew I had been at an R & R Center located in Danang, but I never realized that it was China Beach.

China Beach was a long sandy beach location complete with "life guards". Kind of an ironic term to use under the circumstances. I was very disappointed by the scarcity of females. When I was lucky enough to see one, I was told that the women were probably "donut dollies", and that they never got too friendly with the guys. Donut dollies were women that worked for the Red Cross. They came over voluntarily to help the war effort through USO type work, and were told not to fraternize with the men.

When I landed at the Danang Airport, I saw a lot of activity. There were helicopters and planes everywhere, both military and civilian. It was wild. China Beach had plenty of beer, lots of food, but most of all plenty of rest. I had a chance to see a couple of movies and some live entertainment. A group of entertainers from Korea came in one evening to perform. One guy did some magic tricks...uninteresting, a couple of men did some acrobatics (yawn), but the final act was a longhaired stripper...very interesting. Unfortunately, she didn't do much for us frustrated men. I could see that the married men seemed to feel it the most. Most of us were single kids, and really didn't know what we were missing. After the second day I was so bored that I wanted to go back.

I did spend some time on the beach, and rounded out my R & R enjoying drinking and regular meals. I did manage to get three days of well-needed rest.

When I returned to Camp Eagle, my friend Guillardo, the Battery Clerk, told me that there were three slots open for R & R in Australia. I didn't want to miss that opportunity. So, I went to HQ and complained about that shitty China Beach experience. The Executive Officer at HQ, as luck would have it, was Philip Sheridan. As I mentioned before, he was a good guy. Sheridan was from Dorchester, Massachusetts. When off duty at Fort Campbell, we would occasionally get together, so I knew this was going to be a cinch of a deal. He also gave me the OK for Zok and Pete to take the other two slots. We were all going, and I knew it was going to be a wild time. So within 24 hours, I was repacked, and back on a plane bound for Sidney, Australia. What a way to fight a war!

When we arrived in Sidney, we were bussed over to a store that rented clothes. Yes, believe it or not they rented regular, everyday clothes. We could get suits, pants, shirts and even bathing suits. I rented a couple pair of slacks. Later on when I realized I didn't need slacks, I cut them down and made shorts. The owners, I'm sure, loved us.

Part of the R & R orientation included a lecture on the Australian customs, and discussion of appropriate behavior to ensure that we would be good American representatives. I think they already knew what Americans were like and by the time we left, they knew more about the Screaming Eagles than they cared to know.

Sidney was quite a sight. It felt like being back in the States. No drab olive green and the smells were quite different from Vietnam. The temperature, although warm, was great. We were like kids in a toy store. The hotel, where we stayed, was clean, modern and more importantly...on the beach! People, normal everyday people, were vacationing there, and that made all the difference in the world. It was great to see real people again.

Looking out of our window we could see the pool's shimmering blue water. Our eyes were feasting and our mouths were watering, catching sight of the bikinis lying below. We didn't know what to look at first. The weather was great and the beaches were better, but the women were the best. They were gorgeous and wild.

The best part of Aussie women was their curiosity. They wanted to know everything about America and American men. We were asked if it was true that America was made up of the world's poor. I wanted to liven things up a bit, so I asked if it was true that all Aussies were descendants of convicts and prostitutes. That got their blood flowing. The women got pissed, and the men were insulted.

If they were drinking, they would usually wait until their pint was pretty low before getting up to settle the argument. Then, within a few minutes, a small fight would break out. When the fighting was over, we would all sit back down and start drinking again. They were all so very hospitable, inviting us into their homes for dinner. That was such a treat for us. We really tried to behave ourselves on those occasions to show our appreciation.

Some of the women seemed to have had a lot of experience with American GI's. Once when we were at the hotel, Pete was so drunk that he left the room without getting dressed. I was just getting out of the shower when I heard the door close. I looked out into the hall in time to see Pete trying to get on the elevator. I had no time to get dressed so I ran down the hall naked. When I caught up to him, he was standing in front of the elevator, the door opened and three girls were getting off. They looked at us strangely, shaking their heads.

One of them said, "They must be GI's. They're all alike." Lowering her eyes a bit she went on, "Hey, we've seen that before, and they're all alike too. Just a difference of an inch here or there, ey mate?"

It seemed funny that all GI's basically did the same things when on R & R, and the locals didn't seem to care as long as we were having fun.

We ran out of money within the first week because the drinking and eating never stopped. During the second week the Aussies thought we were great, and they were having so much fun with us, that they started picking up the tabs. The men in the pubs paid for the drinks, and the women would either take us home to eat or would buy us dinner. What a life! We had such a great time that we decided to return after the War. Two weeks went by much too fast. Before we knew it, we were on a plane heading back to Vietnam.

CHAPTER 15

Returning to Vietnam after that trip was terrible.

It was a typically hot evening. We had expected it to be calm and boring. The camp was dark and still, with the exception of generators humming in the background. I'm usually a heavy sleeper, but the crackling sound of a rocket could quickly awaken me.

That's exactly what happened. We started to receive rockets and mortars. It's hard to describe the fear you feel when you're awakened by incoming artillery. That fear, compounded by the feeling of helplessness, is overwhelming. Still, even after all the years that have passed, I am awakened from dreams of that terrifying sound, and find it difficult to go back to sleep. To this day, I sometimes wake to find myself on the floor of my bedroom talking through a mission and wondering, if these nightmares will ever end. I find myself clenching my teeth hoping that the rocket doesn't land close by.

Exploding shells illuminated the darkness through the opening of the bunker. I could smell the musty odor of the bunker and sand bags. Here we were, the children of America, living in a hellhole too far from home.

The sky was bright from burning flames. I thought; there is much too much light. The gooks are going to home into our location.

When the night air filled with shouts of "incoming", our procedure, when under attack, was to get the aircraft off the ground. That was the only real way to protect them. However, this time we decided that it was much safer for us to wait until the attack stopped. To hell with the standard operating procedures. Imagine several helicopters flying nowhere in total darkness, and you can see how dangerous that could be. We decided that our new operating procedure would be to head for the bunkers first, and then maybe, when all the noise was over, take the aircraft off the ground. That was a little easier to handle and made sense to us.

Usually the enemy would fire 15 to 20 rockets, and then go home. This night, an hour had passed, and we were still being shelled. The unrelenting shelling wasn't our only concern. We were also hearing small arms fire out at the perimeter. Not a good sign.

Down on the flight line we could see that one of the aircraft was hit. The sparks ignited something into flames. Then the flames burst into a ball of fire. We all knew that we had to go down to the flight line and put out the fire before it traveled to the other aircraft.

The extinguishers were emptied one after another as the fire blazed on. The enemy now had something for their artillery to zero in on.....a nice bright fire. The enemy shelling was brisk, and going off all around us. There was nothing we could do. The fire went beyond our capabilities. Zok turned to me and yelled.

"Let's get the fuck out of here. I'm going back to the bunkers."

As we dropped into a crater we had hopes that the shelling would let up long enough for us to return to a bunker. We learned that the inside of the bomb crater was filled with water, quite a shocker when it's unexpected. The bottom was filled with water that made the mud knee deep. However, it was our only protection. The barrage of shelling made it necessary for us to crawl most of the way back. We had to escape that barrage because it was aimed directly at the aircraft and right into our path.

The ground was hard, and we had to stay so close to it that the expression 'eating dirt' became literal. We were crawling over sharp rocks that tore at my flesh, and made me bleed from several places because I wasn't wearing a shirt. I was so scared that I didn't feel the pain or notice the bleeding. I remember the small arms fire sounding like fire crackers in the distance. That sound at home meant fun...this was not fun...we learned all new sound and smell associations during this war.

About 100 yards from the bunker, I noticed that one of the guys was still on the flight line trying to extinguish the fire.

I yelled to Zok, "Who the hell is that?"

Zok yelled back, "I don't know."

Once back in the bunker, I fumbled around in the dark looking for a weapon and ammunition. It wasn't easy. I found an M-16 and a few clips. I was hoping that the man on the flight line would have smartened up, and have come back in the bunker. I didn't want to go back down there. No luck. I couldn't help thinking if he was that stupid not to return with us, then he should *be left out to fend for himself.* I really, really didn't want to go back out there. But, I know that if it was me out there, I would have appreciated a helping hand.

I started down the hill to the flight line. I crawled, ran, jumped and whatever I needed to do to make it there alive. When I was close enough, I started yelling to him, but with all the noise he didn't hear me. I decided to make a go for it. I jumped up and ran about thirty yards closer. This time when I yelled, he heard me. Unfortunately, the enemy that broke through the lines also heard me. He stood out like a sore thumb against the fire and then they actually *saw* him. They must have found an opening or a blind spot at the perimeter where they could sneak through. I could hear them shooting and it sounded like they were shooting directly at him. I started firing back hoping to give him some time to get out of the way. We exchanged volleys for a few minutes.

I yelled, "Hey stupid, get the fuck out of there and get to a bunker!"

He was a greenhorn kid. He just arrived in country a few days before, and he had no idea what was going on. I ran up to him, and grabbed him by the back of his pants pulling him to the ground.

"Look, you stupid bastard. You do what I do. When I run, you run, when I go down, you go down. You got that?" He shook his head. "Ok, let's go. I'll provide cover for us."

We ran, dove, and crawled for what seemed like hours. The return firing was fierce. A couple of men had left the bunker to provide cover fire for us. I told the kid to make one last attempt at the bunker when I say, "go". I was almost out of ammunition. There weren't any other choices. We had to make one last run for the bunker. Not only were we in the middle of this firefight, but the rockets and mortars were increasing with intensity.

I didn't see the kid anymore, and hoped he had made it to the bunker. I made one last dash for it myself. As I was running through the bunker entrance a rocket went off real close to me. It was so close that I felt the blast. When I dove through the bunker entrance the blast knocked me on top of Peterson. It was really quite comical. Every time a rocket or mortar started to fall short, the guys did a sort of dance. Everyone would sway to one side away from the opening entrance and after it went off, they would pop back up again. Very bizarre when you think about it. It became very obvious that someone had to go down and take care of the gooks that made it through the perimeter. Bob was the only one who said what we were all thinking.

"We need to take care of those gooks before they join us for breakfast. Guys get your shit together and let's go."

I could tell that they weren't very eager to go, but they went. I can't begin to imagine how many lives were saved by the actions of the men that night during their counter assault.

I came out of the bunker to see if I could watch them make that assault. I was there to give them help if they needed it. I really didn't want to go out there, so I had hoped they didn't need me. It was very dark, and difficult to see them as they zigged and zagged in and around bomb craters and pieces of equipment.

When I heard small arms fire in the distance, I knew they were fully engaged with the Vietnamese. After a few minutes of silence, I saw a silhouette of a man swinging a rifle back and forth as he ran up the hill. It was only one person, and he wasn't wearing a helmet. Shit, what happened? They were all wearing helmets when they left. I grabbed my weapon, jumped up and headed for the silhouette. I went about 20 feet down the hill when I realized that there were two more men behind the silhouette. I said a small prayer, hoping it wasn't VC. It was the men returning, all of them. This was one of many nights we fought all night long. We were certainly relieved when that night was finally over.

That evening during the attack, there was a piece of rocket that flew by my head as I was leaping into the bunker. The next morning I decided to remove that piece of rocket that nearly hit me. I carried it home with me as a reminder, and now have it on a shelf in my home where I look at it every now and then and remember how close I came to being listed on The Wall. The North put up a fierce fight that night. Our hats were off to them. They fought well for their cause. You have to respect that.

CHAPTER 16

Every now and then we were involved in a joint operation working with other branches of the military. One such operation had us providing support at the famous standoff at Khe Sanh. The Marine base at Khe Sanh was under siege for two months. They were surrounded and under heavy attack. To make matters worse the weather was too bad for supplies or additional troops to be flown in to relieve the pressure.

The first indication that we were going someplace different was when we had to report to the medic's tent for vaccinations. I asked the doc for an explanation before I dropped my drawers. The vaccinations were for typhoid fever. They were afraid that the lack of proper storage of human remains would cause a typhoid outbreak. Something to do with rats. I didn't want to think about it. We were told to pack up a couple of hueys with full crews and report to the Marine Air Operations at Phu Bai Airport for possible action at Khe Sanh.

We reported as ordered. The officer in charge was a Major. Most direct officers are shit heads in the States, but usually when they arrive in country they become smart real fast or they would get fragged. This officer was a first class shit head. His first statement to us upon arriving was, "Who the fuck are you, and what are you doing on my base?"

I offered him the verbal orders we received.

"What makes you think that you can help the Marines in a combat situation?"

My answer to him was simple, "I don't know and I don't care, but if you're dismissing us from the operation, please sign a statement to that affect and we'll be out of your way."

"Don't you get smart with me, mister. My Marines can out fly and out shoot you pukes. What makes you think we need you?"

About that time a Lt. Colonel walked into the tent, and walked directly over to me, shook my hand.

He said, "Boy am I glad to have you guys here. We really need the help." Then turning to the Major, "Do you know that the 101" have flown twice the amount of HELO sorties in this area with a smaller contingency of aircraft than we have. They know this area inside and out. Major, you should plan on utilizing their expertise while we have them."

He then moved over to a couple of Marine fighter support pilots, and began going over their charts. The Major was definitely not happy at the reception we were given by his Commander. He immediately turned to the Sergeant, and told him that he was going to the head. After the Major left the operations tent the Sergeant came over to me.

"Don't worry about him. He's only been in country for a couple of months, and his experience in the Marines has mainly been as a supply officer. So far he's been a fuck up when it comes to operations. We've been bailing his ass out since he got here. If he keeps this shit up nobody will help him out of his next bind."

The Major returned and asked everyone to be seated. I know for a fact that he would have been a complete asshole if his LTC had left. He started briefing us on the operation and issued the assignments. Of course he gave us the shit part of the mission. It was our job to transport all of the nonessential supplies. We were also placed last in the formation. The explanation for this, being Army, we didn't have any idea how the Marines operated. Whatever!

When all was said and done, we had our aircraft loaded, fueled and finally in the air.

Flying into Khe Sanh was a bitch. The first two Marine helicopters that were flying in formation needed to open up due to weather conditions. Then they saw how dangerous it was, and decided to turn back. They made a wise decision. Consequently several C-130's filled with supplies refused to go in without the gun ship support that was promised.

The weather was miserable. At Khe Sanh, they were having a mix of light rain and fog, which made following other aircraft in some type of formation impossible.

Every now and then we would lose sight of the aircraft flying right in front of us. It wasn't a very smart way to fly because one of the worst things that could happen, happened. We lost sight of the formation completely.

We were on our own so we decided to drop back even further to help avoid an in air collision. Pete decided that we should try to find that base by ourselves. We flew in the fog for a while. I don't think any of the pilots was up to date in instrument flying. We had the coordinates of the base, and without the other aircraft to worry about, we wanted to give it a try. Then just as we started to say, *"That's it, we're turning back."* a hole opened, and the base was almost below us. We flew to the closest clearing, maneuvering our way and set down.

The crew began unloading throwing the supplies off the aircraft onto the ground. A few Marines came over to help. About fifteen minutes later everyone stopped unloading. I noticed some of the Marines talking. We needed to get out of there as soon as possible. One of the Marines came over to my window.

"I'm the CO here. Where the fuck is the ammunition and food we need? What the fuck is this shit?"

I knew he was looking for the supplies that were loaded on the other aircraft and obviously those aircraft were not going to make it. I just shrugged my shoulders, waved my arms and signaled for the crew to get back into the aircraft.

If they didn't want what we had, I wanted out of there. The aircraft was a perfect target for the VC and the small arms fire was increasing every second we were on the ground. The only way out for us was straight up. We spiraled as high as we could, and then headed for the fog to gain protection. When we reached 1500 feet, we broke through the top of the fog, pointed our nose down and headed for home.

My nerves were finally starting to settle down. My hands were shaking again, and I was in a sweat, but it wasn't from the heat. This was another new feeling for me. I didn't think that this feeling would ever happen to me. We started to see some breaks in the clouds as we headed for home base.

Zok on the intercom, "I see an aircraft on the ground at 9:00 O'clock. The blades are not turning, and the men are outside. It looks like they're setting up a perimeter."

After several attempts to raise them on the radio, we called the Marine operations radio to see if they had a downed aircraft in the area. They did confirm that they had a downed aircraft, but very reluctantly. The Operations Major, who by now was being referred to as Major Fuck-up, had not notified anyone of his downed aircraft. That was a "major fuck up".

We decided to go in, and see if we could help. We no more wanted to help that self-righteous pompous ass Marine Major out of this jam, but we weren't really thinking of him. We were concerned about his men on the ground. We were there for the combat Marines, our fellow soldiers. Fuck the Major.

We buzzed the aircraft a couple of times to see if we would draw some enemy fire. We were hoping that the men could give us some sort of a sign. I guessed that their popping green smoke meant that it was clear to land, but who could tell. Prior to landing, I told the crew to throw out the shit we were carrying to make room. Once we landed, I had everyone load any ammunition or food that remained on the grounded aircraft into ours. We could then take those supplies, and try to get back to Khe Sanh.

We decided that we were going to try and give those Marines what they needed to survive. We didn't know that Major Fuck up ordered the Marine helicopters back to base and stopped the operation.

As we landed next to the other aircraft the Marines came over and jumped in. They wanted to get out of there as fast as possible. The pilot in command of the other aircraft was a Captain. He came over to Pete's window.

He yelled, "Let's get this aircraft off the ground."

We didn't pay attention to him motioning to the men to start transferring the supplies. I turned to that Captain and yelled at him.

"I suggest you get off your ass and help if you want to get out of here any time soon.

He wasn't pleased, and became more furious when he realized that we were going back to Khe Sanh to deliver the supplies. There was no question in my mind that we had to go back to deliver these desperately needed supplies. We couldn't conceive of abandoning those men without even trying to give them some help. There was no one else around to do it. So we headed back to that dreaded area. Later thinking about the whole experience, I guess, the pilot was correct in not wanting to return. We could have had several well-trained officers killed, beside ourselves, for a few enlisted Marines. Bullshit! A life is a life.

This time the flight wasn't as easy as it was the first time. We did find our way in, except this time when we broke through the fog we were in the middle of a raging battle. As we jockeyed around looking for a position to land, several rounds went through the windshield.

I noticed one area of the compound that looked clear. We flew the huey over, and set it down. I had a few minutes to digest the scene. My God, I thought, these men will never get out of here alive. Half of the location was a bomb crater with fatalities located at different locations throughout. I felt a rush of hot air pass through my body. My face was red hot, we had to get out of there and fast. If we lost our aircraft now, we were dead meat.

This time all of the men including the Marine flight crew helped unload the supplies throwing them off as fast as humanly possible. Several more rounds passed through the aircraft. It seemed like the aircraft was the bull's eye on a target. Most of the firing was aimed at us. As far as we knew nothing crucial on the aircraft had been hit. With both M-60s firing, and both barrels turning red hot, we pulled pitch hard. The nose pointed to the ground, and the blades pulled us straight forward. Although we exceeded a couple of redlines on the panel, and received many rounds right through the aircraft, we made it out.

On our way back, I couldn't help but think of the men we left back at that camp, imagining what was in store for them. I didn't envy them at all. The ride back was beginning to become somewhat calm and comfortable. I was a little premature in letting the adrenaline ebb, because the oil temperature lights and warning signals started to come on one at a time. Pete leaned over and tapped the instrument gauge to get my attention.

"Russo, what do you think? Can we make it?"

"Zok, hang out and see if there is oil leaking outside of the aircraft."

Just about that time the controls started to gyrate uncontrollably. We must have taken a hit in the hydraulics. The controls were hydraulic, and the system would shut down without fluid. Also, the backup system must have been damaged because nothing was working. This meant, controlling the aircraft would be very difficult.

Zok on the intercom, "I can see some oil dripping down the side of the cowling, it looks like its red."

That was the proof we needed. Hydraulic fluid. I called to Zok.

"You're needed up front to sit on the collective to help control the aircraft."

The collective is a control that allows us to lift the aircraft, and change the pitch of the main blades to lift off the ground or land safely. Since the collective was operated by hydraulics, the collective and cyclic would be lost.

"OK Zok, when I tell you to push it down, you push it down or sit on it. It needs to be stabilized."

That would help us to land, at least that was what we were hoping. I checked the map and remembered noticing an artillery setup in the area. This seemed as good a place as any to try and land. With Zok sitting on the collective arm and Pete and I pulling on the cyclic, the aircraft started to slowly descend. We radioed control asking them to contact artillery operations to let them know we were in trouble and landing at one of their camps. I didn't know who they were, but I didn't care at that point.

The aircraft came in ever so slowly, but it just wouldn't land. It leaned to one side. Pete and I pulled the stick in the opposite direction to keep it straight. When we hit the ground, it kept lifting off in a bouncing motion. We decided to drop the setting on the turbine to decrease the RPM's of the engine and main rotor. I could smell burning hydraulic fluid as it sprayed over the engine. On the next try the aircraft stayed on the ground long enough for us to shut down the engine. There is an old pilot's expression, "any landing that we can walk away from is a good landing", and we were thankful for this one.

We went right to work trying to fix the aircraft. One of the oil lines was severed, and both hydraulic lines were hit. After surveying the damage, we radioed our unit and explained what we needed. The Maintenance Officer decided to send a turbine expert to take a better look at the engine. Later that day another mechanic arrived with the parts needed. He made the repairs, purged the hydraulic lines, inspected the engine, and gave us the go ahead for a one-time flight back to Camp Eagle. Before liftoff, all non-essential equipment was transferred back to another aircraft to lighten the load. For safety reasons, one person flew the damaged Huey back alone. When we arrived at Camp Eagle, we had a message waiting for us from the Marine TLC Operations Commander. He thanked us for, in his words, "a job well done" and recommended us for citations.

CHAPTER 17

The repetition of flying the same type of mission day after day was starting to take its toll on our sanity. I asked flight operations to give us a change in venue. We needed to do something different. Flight operations granted our request, and assigned our aircraft to support a Naval Patrol Boat on the Perfume River. We were to work as a team with the Navy patrolling the waterways.

It seemed that gunboats, while on patrol, were ambushed at least once a day. The Marines, who were in direct support of the Navy, usually flew that type of operation. However, since they were having their own problems with some of their base camps. The Marine LTC Commander requested we fly visual support for them providing artillery support when needed. This was an easy job for us because flying visual recon was our specialty.

We flew into the vicinity of the gunboats, and made radio contact. After a few days the missions became routine. We flew ahead of the gunboats checking for a potential ambush.

It was during one of those *typical* patrols that the VC out-foxed us. As the first gunboat started to patrol several miles ahead of the second vessel, we turned back to make sure the second boat was OK. Then we were asked to check a riverbed at a turn that was just ahead of the lead boat. We were told that local fishermen had reported seeing some VC at the bend. We pulled ahead, made a 360 turn and dropped down to tree top level. The bend was a haven of high elephant grass, and was very thickly covered. The river's dark brown color meshed with the high elephant grass. The combination provided great camouflage for anyone trying to hide. As we dropped into the clearing of high grass, we became the targets of heavy ground fire.

"Gun Boat 3, this is Eagle Gunner seven-niner-six. We are receiving ground fire from both river banks, over."

The VC had positioned themselves on both sides of the river, and were waiting in prey for the gunboats. We decided to call artillery while directing the boats to stay clear of the friendly fire. They acknowledged our message and complied. We directed the artillery by flying the arch. After bombarding the area with twenty to thirty 105-howitzer rounds, the area looked secure enough to fly through. We flew through the area several times without spotting any sign of movement, but spotted several VC bodies.

"Gun Boat 3, Eagle Gunner, no additional movement sighted. All looks secured, over."

"This is Gun Boat 3, we roger that, and are moving into the area with both vessels, out."

The Gun Boats were about halfway through the area when they started to receive small arms fire. After all that howitzer firepower, there were still VC alive and ready to continue the fight. The number two boat was then hit with a rocket. The boat ignited instantly. The other boat came in and was in the process of picking up the men. We gave cover by firing into the grassy areas. We supplied as much cover fire as possible.

The problem with fighting the VC was that we never saw them. Our cover fire was not enough, because the aid boat was also hit and caught fire. We now had a pretty good idea where the firepower was coming from, but we couldn't attack. We needed to protect the men while they made their way to shore. As we hovered over the men a barrage of small arms began firing at us penetrating the aircraft skin at several locations. We fired back, with several volleys. The firefight went on for what seemed like hours, when in reality it was only about 15 minutes.

When flying directly into the oncoming rounds, we could actually see the rounds coming at us. They looked like little white lights, appearing so harmless, but they could be so devastating. I called Div-arty requesting they fire smoke for cover on the right riverbank. They complied. I needed it to hide the men while they made their way to shore. We then received several rounds through the windshield and more into the body of the aircraft. So far, no one was hit, and the aircraft was still flying.

We hovered and returned fire over the men as they slowly made their way back to land. We radioed back to command several times during the action asking for assistance in picking up the men. This particular aircraft was not made for carrying weight. We were flying one of the new Hughes aircraft made for observation with only defense weapons installed. We were strictly reconnaissance and support, an OH-6A.

Pete's aircraft was the first to make it to the location. They came in and strafed the area several times with machine gun fire before they tried to land for a pickup. His aircraft happened to be the Artillery Command Ship for artillery, and was in the area.

"Eagle Gunner seven-niner-six, I am going to try and make a pickup. Keep your eyes open."

The huey then made its way for the extraction. We could see the M-60 smoking as they went in. Then we received a message.

"We are engulfed in small arms fire from all sides. Seven-niner-six, we're receiving heavy fire. Can you help us out with some cover fire?"

The next message was "MAYDAY, MAYDAY, this is Eagle Gunner Command going down two miles south on the Perfume River. (*Two minutes later*) This is Eagle Gunner Command, we're leaving the aircraft for cover, out."

As we flew overhead we were running at 110 knots, and could see the Navy boat crew, and now the Div-arty flight crew in bomb craters. They were fighting off what looked to be Vietcong gorillas. The action was hot. We came in and gave some fire support, but we kept moving in and out of the zone full speed to avoid becoming another downed aircraft. The Vietcong were so brazen that they were out in the open, and they were trying to cross the river. It was unheard of for the Vietcong to expose themselves unless they felt they had a decisive victory.

I called for more artillery to help hold back the VC from crossing the river, and asked Command for desperately needed ground troops. We flew as close as possible trying to protect the men by giving as much cover fire as possible. Suddenly, one of our audio alarms started to scream indicating a loss in oil pressure. Then almost immediately the engine RPM indicator went to zero. We were in big trouble! We were partially over the water, with enough forward air speed that could place us over land, and put us as close to our men as possible. As soon as we hit the ground I started yelling.

"Get out. Take your weapons, move, move, move."

The training drummed into me took over. I threw all of my gear out, and jumped out after it. We were lucky enough to be in an upright position when we performed the emergency landing. I directed everyone to get into some type of cover and away from the aircraft. I knew that the aircraft would be the VC's prime target once grounded.

To this day, I can still remember the smell of the elephant grass mixed with the scent of gunpowder and my perspiration. My heart was pounding so loud that I was certain it could be heard by everyone even above the gunfire and of course my hands were shaking as before. I hated that my body would do this to me. I felt like I had no control.

I crawled back to the aircraft to remove the emergency radio and the survival pack. The emergency radio transmitted on a high frequency. A couple of minutes later I was receiving a transmission from an Air Force jet somewhere in the area at 15,000 feet. We asked him to make sure our unit was notified to send help in the form of ground troops. We were notified that our unit had already started sending in help. He also stated that his aircraft did not have any weapons that could help us.

"Sorry guys, I guess you're on your own for now."

We were receiving small arms fire from every direction and were completely surrounded. I looked over to Zok in the other bomb crater. He looked at me, and we both started laughing. I don't know why. I guess it was just one of those crazy things you do when your nerves are shot and your ass has had it. I was thinking that this was it!

I heard a noise behind me, and when I looked, there were several men in black pajamas working their way toward us. I took a couple of shots in their direction. It stopped them for a moment, but again, they started to come. This time they were shooting as they came. We didn't have much ammunition, so we had to be very careful not to waste a shot. I yelled to the men.

"Try to save your ammo, only take shots that count."

Just then, from the corner of my eye, I saw a black blur coming at me. I quickly turned and fired. Charlie dropped to the ground. Behind him were two more. Again, I fired several times. They also went down and didn't get up. It was a momentary relief. I heard a scream from one of the bomb craters. A boat crew member was hit and yelling for help. That was all I needed. I was so frightened; my hands were shaking more than ever; and I was starting to hyperventilate. I started telling myself *"calm down, calm down, calm down, take it easy, relax, calm down..."* It helped a little but not much.

The shooting stopped, and it became very quiet, too quiet. I picked up my radio to see if I could raise some help. I heard a voice.

"Eagle Gunner seven-niner-six, come in."

I thought, thank God.

"Where the hell are you guys, over."

Then, fifty yards to my right in a crater, members of the boat crew started firing. I could hear the enemy firing back. Trying to move around inside a crater half filled with water was nearly impossible. I was covered with mud from head to toe. When you realize that in the next moment you may be dead, the minutes can seem like hours.

Then it happened. They started a direct frontal attack with a vengeance. They were so fiercely intent on killing us at any cost, that they were performing this attack in the open and in full daylight. That was unprecedented during my time in Vietnam. They must have calculated that our ammunition reserves were low, and they were right. We were close to being out. Several VC's came straight at me. I shot twice, and they went down.

Unfortunately, a couple of the boat crew members were now hit. I knew they needed medical help soon. Our situation was looking grim. There was nothing we could do. I have never felt so helpless. I had hoped that help would arrive before we ran out of ammunition.

Again, all was quiet. Now I fully realized what was meant by *the quiet before the storm*. I just knew this was it. How do you prepare yourself to die? Then I heard the wonderful sound of huey blades overhead with guns blazing and rockets firing. The next thing I felt was a grunt jumping into the crater next to me.

"How ya doing? Need a little help?"

It was a grunt with a medic following close behind. I quickly pointed him toward the direction of the wounded, and off he went. Five minutes later, men from the 101st were standing all around me. Aircraft were coming in two at a time. Men were being off loaded everywhere. It was like being back at base camp. There were so many men and so much equipment everywhere. What a great feeling! Noise, aircraft, guns, men, it was great! I could finally breath again. Full of adrenaline and strengthened by the presence of my fellow members of the 101st, I jumped up like nothing had happened.

"Ya, that's right. We gave them a run for their money, and we weren't bull shitting around with them. If you waited a few more minutes, we would have knocked the shit out of the rest of them......Airborne!!"

The adrenaline was flowing.

The battle was over...nothing to worry about. To reassure the guys, I told them what a great job they had done. While inside I was shaking, crying, praying and hoping that nobody could tell what I was really feeling.

Looking back, I'm sure everyone was feeling the same way. I was mentally drained. I find myself waking up in the middle of that battle, trying to catch my breath, as I did back then. I have carried those emotional scars for a very long time.

Today I sometimes look at people I meet, who are so petty and self-absorbed, and I find myself frustrated beyond belief by their small mindedness. Such myopic views that show how little they really know about life. So much is taken for granted, and they don't remotely realize the price of their privilege.

A couple of the empty aircraft came in and picked up the wounded. For that moment, all was well. Later that day they would airlift the damaged aircraft out along with the dead VC soldiers. The damage was deep. Two Naval crew were killed; two of our aircraft crew were injured; and eight VC bodies were found. The final count of ammunition showed less than fifty rounds between 12 men. My 'Band of Brothers' gave me back my life that day, but the nightmares from the memory of it have robbed me peaceful nights ever since.

CHAPTER 18

Every now and then the war would seem to quiet down and with that, the enemy would surprise us and rear its ugly head.

It was early morning and the temperature was already up to 109 degrees Fahrenheit. Everyone was busy doing their job. The aircraft were being inspected, fueled and routine maintenance was being performed. Nothing irregular for a combat zone. In the maintenance tent, we usually have a two-way radio on in the event one of our aircraft needed to communicate with us. This particular morning we noticed an unusual amount of traffic on the radio. We could also hear our artillery firing toward the northwest every few minutes.

This morning the air was especially still and hot. Most of us were sweating from just doing minor physical work, and we had no fat to sweat off. Cold sodas were scarce, and the water tasted like shit. Our water supply was pumped out of a swamp, and mixed with chlorine and other chemicals to purify it, then mixed with cool aid...it was garbage.

Judging from the heavier than normal amount of chatter on the radio this morning, we could tell that there was a large operation taking place somewhere in the A Shau Valley. We didn't know exactly where the Valley was located, but we knew that it was thick jungle. We could tell that several aircraft were communicating from that zone.

Around 8:00 AM, we received a call from Artillery Command. They wanted us to make a visual reconnaissance flight in an area somewhere in the A Shau Valley. Command was sending two artillery men for coordination and direction of artillery if needed for ground operations support.

The NVA had several Russian made anti-aircraft fifty caliber guns set up somewhere in the operations area of the Valley. When the two artillery men arrived, they informed us that those anti-aircraft weapons downed several aircraft this morning alone. Surprisingly, the two men were the Battalion Commander Col. Pohl and his Command Sgt. Major Browning. It was up to us to find the location of those weapons, and have artillery put them out of commission.

As we were carrying our gear out to the aircraft, we ritually tossed a coin to see who was going to get dressed first, and start the aircraft.

That morning, we had a feeling that we would be seeing a lot of action on this flight, so we decided to wear every piece of protective gear, and take every weapon we could find. We were issued 38 Special handguns, and we had previously bargained on the black market for an M-1 Carbine and French automatic weapons. We wore our chest protectors, ballistic flight helmets, armor-plated seating, asbestos gloves and uniforms. We were hoping all of this was unnecessary, but subconsciously somehow I realized we would need it all.

The Battalion Commander was a full Colonel. He approached the aircraft with a chart in his hand, and showed us where he thought the guns would be set up. He climbed aboard the sister aircraft, and we both cranked up and headed for the jungle.

The radio waves were filled with ground to air operations chatter. As we approached the area where one of the downed aircraft was spotted, we flew by at a full clip. The Colonel wanted to see where the aircraft was downed while he tried to determine where the firing was coming from. We didn't see any immediate evidence of enemy guns. So the Colonel ordered us to make a 360 turn, and directed us to a clearing.

Over the intercom, "Take a look in that area."

Pete and I were in the first helicopter that approached the site. The second aircraft which carried the Battalion Commander and the Sgt Major was flown by Lt. Baker and WO Kusterman. For Pete and I, this was our first mission together after I returned from LZ Jane. We decided to go back about a mile and hedge hop at 100 knots into the clearing. This would give us the element of surprise, and hopefully the ability to see them long before they saw us.

We explained our strategy to the Colonel. He really didn't want to hear it because he was in a hurry. We decided to do it our way anyhow. Speaking through the intercom, I told everyone to pay very close attention as we dropped into that area.

"Keep a sharp eye out for those guns, and make sure you don't hit our other aircraft."

We began our run dropping down going through and over the trees. Every now and then we would see some of our ground troops in small clearings.

"A couple more trees and we'll be in the open. Men, get ready. Keep your eyes open."

The Commander's aircraft followed closely behind. As we dropped into the clearing, all hell broke loose. Our aircraft, which was going 120 knots forward, was almost stopped dead in midair from the bombardment of 50 caliber rounds penetrating her. The windshield was completely blown into splinters. The shrapnel from the floor was flying throughout, and none of the controls would respond. In a matter of seconds the 50 caliber rounds sent us to the ground.

The aircraft spun to the left, and slid almost like a glider. The main rotor blades started chopping down the trees as we descended and finally broke apart like the twigs they had just chopped. The ground came up to meet us with the terrible sound of metal and earth meshing together.

Then, as fast as it started, it stopped. All was eerily quiet, except for the spinning of the gyrocompass and some small radio chatter that sounded muffled. I felt like I was transported to another world. I was dazed, and everything seemed dreamlike. The gyrocompass and the radio echoed through my brain. I didn't know whether or not I should move. My body felt like it had shattered along with the aircraft. My chest protector had metal stuck into it, and my chin was bleeding. I looked over where Pete had been, and he wasn't there. He was ejected from his seat on impact. I spotted him getting up from the ground. He was walking, and that was good. I climbed out of the aircraft to see the command aircraft going down some 50 feet away. I tried to compose myself, so I could check the crew in our aircraft before we headed for the command ship.

We found the command aircraft on its side. I opened the door to Kusterman's side of the aircraft. He was halfway between the seat and what was left of the floor housing. Blood was coming from his mouth. I knew that meant that he was seriously injured. Reality was beginning to settle in as I became more aware of my surroundings.

We were starting to smell smoke. This was one of our biggest fears, fire. My first thought was to get the hell away before the aircraft blew. I moved very slowly at first. Everything seemed like it was happening in slow motion. I'm sure we were all in shock.

The aircraft was leaning over almost completely blocking off the side opening. It actually looked like it was going to roll over. I could see Zok and Pfefferman. They were already carrying the Colonel away from the aircraft, and were headed back for the Sgt. Major.

I felt myself to see if I had any injuries. My leg was injured, but I really didn't feel the pain then probably as a result of the shock. I didn't realize it at the time, but I had taken a round off of my chest protector, and it slapped my chin and exited out through my flight helmet. I was still trying to get out of that daze.

The full impact of what had happened was beginning to sink in, and I decided that we needed to get everyone away from the aircraft before it became fully engulfed by fire. I climbed up and into the aircraft to see if I could get Kusterman out. He was wedged between his seat and the floor, and his seat belt was jammed locked. I needed a knife to cut the belt.

"Zok, I need a knife. Kusterman's seat belt is jammed. Do you have anything that cuts?"

Zok always kept a blade by his side. I don't know why I didn't remember that. He came over, and cut the belt. I didn't know about the others, but I was still very confused and probably still in shock, but we finally managed to get him out.

The smoke was quickly replaced by flames, and we had one more person to get out, the other gunner, Bill. The aircraft had rolled over a little more to the ground. Zok and I made our way to the other side of the aircraft. Zok slid under the small opening between the ground and the aircraft.

He yelled back to me, "He's unconscious and I can't get his safety belt off."

Now the flames were getting very high and hot. The ammunition on the opposite side of the aircraft was going off from the heat. I slid myself down between the openings with Zok. Pfefferman found a way to reach in, and was able to cut Bill's safety belt free. We dragged him out and away from the plane. We were lucky, within a few minutes the entire aircraft was completely engulfed causing the aircraft to roll directly over on the location we had just vacated. A few minutes longer and we all would have been toast.

Within a few minutes ground troops appeared, and provided us with protection. Their Medic came over and started to work on Bill. After a couple of minutes he turned to us and said, "This guy is dead. He was probably killed from the crash."

Bill Bader was one of those guys that everybody liked.

Zok said, "You're not going to believe this, but last night Bill passed each of us a beer and said, if I die tomorrow, I want you guys to have a party. I'm not kidding, a party."

I said, "That's wild. Why would he say such a thing? Do you think he had a premonition?"

It was certainly strange, but to honor Bill's request, we did have that party. I knew he had a girl back home waiting for him. They had planned a wedding on his return. I felt very sorry for her loss, and the end to all of her plans.

The Medic checked the Colonel, Sgt. Major and Kusterman. "The Colonel and Sgt. Major are both dead. The other pilot is alive, barely. I think he has internal injuries, and is bleeding deep inside of his lungs. We need a Med-O-Vac now if this pilot is going to live."

We scrambled to find ground troops with a radio and immediately called for a Med-O-Vac unit. We told the voice on the other end that the Med-O-Vac was for a full Bird Colonel. That usually sent requests into high gear.

A Med-O-Vac helicopter came in almost instantly. Before I knew it a team of doctors and nurses from the local MASH Unit were examining all of us. Then we were sent on to the Hospital Ship, Repose, for additional treatment. That day we lost several aircraft and some ten men before the guns were found and silenced. A very high price to pay for a few guns.

CHAPTER 19

Zok, Pete, and I were hoping to stay close to home base for the remainder of our time. We often heard stories about men getting killed during their last week or sometimes last day in country. We didn't want that to happen to us. We had survived so much trauma to go now would really be unfair. However, we did have to go out on daily missions, but we tried to keep them as peaceful as possible. During this period, after completing a mission and before returning to base, we found other things to do with the remainder of the day. We found a beach that was safe, or at least as safe as one can get in Vietnam. We would fly in and lie out in the sun or just take a cool refreshing swim.

The Gulf of Tomkin was our swimming hole. I remember how salty the water was, and the seashells were so different from those I was used to on the East Coast of the US. Sea Horse and periwinkle shells were more the norm. The beaches were naturally sandy and fairly clean, considering we were in a war zone. The sun was so hot that it would bake the shells to a point where they would feel like plastic. I took a few of these shells home with me to show my family, a peaceful remembrance from war torn Vietnam.

We were basically on our own at the beach. There were no other US personnel in the area. No one to be on guard when swimming, except one of us. The sun was very strong even in the late hours of the day. I can remember the color of the water being a beautiful turquoise, but it was always rough. I loved to feel the stinging of the salt after drying off, it reminded me of being home on the beach. Later in the day when the sun would start to set, my sunburn would give me the chills.

For a brief moment in time I could really forget the war. I would get a feeling of inner peace and relaxation. It's hard to imagine, men of my age having this type of feeling. Of course not many men my age had to live with death every day. It was all part of growing up in a combat unit. My hands would stop shaking when I was feeling this inner peace. I would see a jetliner high above and wish that I was on it heading almost anywhere.

I could tell that the war was taking its toll on me. I was like everyone else; I wouldn't admit that I was beginning to feel differently towards life. When we had a chance to party, we did, and with more gusto than we had in the past, if that were possible. It was our way of enjoying being alive and trying to forget the horrors we had seen. On the surface, to most people, we looked like we were just a bunch of crazy paratroopers. If they had any understanding of what we had been through, they would have realized that we were just coping.

Flying support for the Navy Patrol Boat Squadron had its rewards. Occasionally, they would invite us to spend time on their barge. The barge was made with a helipad on the deck and docks for the gunboats with several barge living units strung together giving the whole setup the appearance of being one large vessel.

It worked out well for us. We could swim or just watch movies in the afternoon. They had all of the comforts of home. Patrolling the waterways in Vietnam was no picnic. The gunboats were wide-open prey for every hit and run by Vietcong near the water. Given the choice, it was not something I would have liked doing.

One of the most enjoyable days we spent, was aboard the aircraft carrier Coral Sea. It wasn't a ship; it was a city on water. One morning after flying support for Navy jets, we were invited to return to the aircraft carrier for lunch. We thought it would be fun meeting the pilots we flew support for each day. After receiving a fix from one of the pilots, we headed out to sea. When we hit an hour of flying time, I started to get a little nervous because we hadn't spotted the carrier yet, and fuel was beginning to get a little low. Slowly, out on the ocean, in a distance, a dot appeared on the horizon and as the dot grew bigger, a ship started to appear. At first we could see white engine wash, then this mountain started to grow up in front of us. We were used to flying ten feet off of the ground so as we came closer the vessel looked like a mountain emerging from out of the water.

We needed permission to land, at first their flight operations, refused us. Apparently their radar wasn't picking us up because we were flying low. We were lucky that the ship didn't have the automatic weapons protection system on. I understand that this system automatically picks out any target below the gunnels line and disables it immediately.

We were allowed to land after we received instructions on how to land on a carrier. We were directed to hover to an elevator that carried us, including our aircraft, below deck. The ship's crew looked at us like we were aliens. We crawled out of our aircraft dusting ourselves off, tired from the days work. I guess this crew hadn't seen many soldiers like us before. Land operations and heavy ground combat equipment were not part of their experience.

A Lieutenant came over to us and asked, "Which one of you is the pilot in command?"

Nobody acknowledged.

"Whoever it is, the Captain wants to see you on the bridge immediately."

A couple of us followed the Lieutenant to the bridge. On the way up, I couldn't help but notice how clean and luxurious it was on the ship. Everything shined and smelled nice. These accommodations were not something we were used to. As we entered the bridge, I noticed the clean pressed uniforms, nicely shined shoes and even a cook dressed in a white uniform serving coffee. I thought, it must be a great life, as we stood there in stark comparison with our wrinkled and sweaty flight suits.

The Captain approached us, placed his hands on his hips and just took a long look. I then knew that he was not part of a welcoming committee.

"I should have known I would be dealing with the likes of you. You hot shot Paratroopers think you're winning this war all by yourselves."

We said nothing.

He continued, "Don't you know the proper procedure for approaching and landing on a ship? Don't you realize that our guns automatically fire on anything that is approaching our ship?" He knew he had a captive audience on the bridge so, he continued with a vengeance, "You people, were flying below fifty feet. Our radar didn't detect you, but our guns did. If it weren't for our pilots telling flight OPS that you were en route, you would have been shot down Now, I wouldn't care if you were shot down, but I do care that it would go on my record; and another thing, how stupid could you be flying this far out to sea. I'll bet you don't even have enough fuel to return. What would you have done if you ran into bad weather? Now, I don't know what business you have here, but I expect you to complete it, refill your tanks and leave, understand?"

We stood without blinking an eye. "Yes, Sir" we then turned and left the bridge as fast as we could.

It took us some time to find our way back to the hanger area. I found the men in a huddle with a couple of jet pilots. They were trying to outdo each other in war stories. Then the pilots give them directions to the mess area, and one was explaining that they had nightly movies and told us where they were held.

When we found the mess hall, it was huge, no canned hot dogs here! It was absolutely amazing. That day happened to be Friday, and we were told on Fridays they offer varieties of seafood. The entrees read like a New York restaurant: steak to order, lobster, steamed shrimp, and some type of roast. There were five side dishes. We couldn't believe our eyes. They had fresh tomatoes, strawberries and several other fresh foods. Foods that we hadn't seen in almost a year.

I asked one of the naval crew if they really are paid for combat duty and given credit for being in a combat zone. He said, "of course." Here they were living in luxury, while the rest of us were living in nothing more than a hole in the ground. Unbelievable! We were definitely in the wrong branch of the military.

I filled my plate with so much food that it was falling out and onto the tray. I couldn't remember when I had a meal that great. It was then we decided to radio back and tell Div-arty operations that we were having problems with the aircraft, and it would probably take a couple of days before we could become airborne. We had made the call and then I decided to see where the ship was positioned. At that point I realized that we were too far out at sea to return to land. I knew what the Captain said, but hey, it wasn't our fault that his ship was too far out from land for us to return. Besides, the opportunity was too good to pass up. That night we saw the film *Hawaii*, and there was plenty of beer and snacks to go around. What a way to fight a war! We were there for three days, and were they glorious.

The following day, the carrier was in a close enough position for us to reach land. Before we knew it, we were once again landing at Camp Eagle. It was like we never left. It was around lunchtime and our great chefs were serving a choice of hot C-rations or cold C-rations. What a treat!

When we were on board ship, we tried to start an exchange program where men from the ship would stay in our living quarters while some of us took their places on ship. Swapping places with us for a few days, would give them invaluable land/combat experience. We tried to sell it as an educational adventure. Not surprised, there were no takers...who would be that stupid...still you can dream.

Most of the men that deployed with the Division were now in country several months and were beginning to get a little antsy. The life between missions was boring. We either played cards or drank. To keep our sanity, we turned to doing crazy antics.

We decided that our next project was the building of a still. Yes, a vessel for concocting alcoholic beverages. Billy Rae was born in the Ozark Mountains, and had a passing familiarity with still construction. He figured out a way to make an electric still. It was a short-lived project ending with it burning up, but before it blew, we had some heavy hangovers.

Tony Barrera was Mexican, and was always receiving care packages of Mexican food and snacks from home. As soon as he would receive a package, he would lock it up in his homemade cabinet figuring it was safe until he returned from the day's flight mission. Several of the men figured out a way to get into his cabinet, take some of his food, then relock the cabinet and wait for him to return. He would sit and look at his locker trying to figure out how the food was taken. Now the men wouldn't clean him out. They would take just enough so he would know that it was missing. This went on for quite a while until he figured out a way to burglar proof his cabinet.

One of the biggest and best ideas came from Peterson. He suggested that we have a barbeque. Having a barbecue doesn't sound like much, but trying to have one in a war zone with steaks, ice, fresh vegetables, lots of cold beer and charcoal was not easy. That was the best part of it. It seemed impossible, so now we had a challenge to occupy us.

We all sat down and did some brainstorming. We needed everything. To start with, we needed charcoal. That was fairly easy. There were Vietnamese merchants that made charcoal from burned trees. All we had to do was go out and buy a few pounds. The Think Tank was beginning to boil. We would fly out to one of the Merchant Marine freighters anchored outside of the harbor and make a deal. The Merchant Mariners were always ready to deal. Obviously they were a lot better at this than we were. They wanted Russian AK assault rifles and US uniforms. The merchant ships had no problem bringing these guns back into the States. They were hardly checked once docked. In return, we would bargain for steaks, lettuce, tomatoes and strawberries.

One of our biggest problems was ice. There was an ice house located near Camp Eagle. It was at the Seabees' base. Pete volunteered to get the ice. He was committed to do whatever it took to get the ice. It didn't matter if he had to steal or whatever he had to trade to get it, he would. He was ready to deal. After all, it wasn't like we were trying to get a refrigerator!

It was easier than we thought. Pete invited the Seabees to the party in return for the ice. However, he threw in a few facts that weren't really true. He told them that we had the nurses from the two MASH Units, and the Donut Dollies from China Beach at the Danang Base. I think it was the Donut Dollies that clinched the deal.

The ice came in large blocks 6' long x 2' wide x 10" thick. Peterson stacked four high in the back seat and three high in the front seats. He was actually sitting on them while driving the jeep. Peterson had quite a trip trying to get all of the ice back all by himself. The ice kept sliding out of the jeep. Every time the jeep would bounce, a slab of ice would slide out and onto the road. Pete was trying to sit on the ice to keep it from moving and the harder he tried, the more it slid off and into the road. It was a long cold ride back to camp. I think that most of the men he passed on the road had a good laugh. It was a sight.

The final ingredient that would guarantee the success of any party was beer. We wanted to have enough beer for everyone. We were all given beer rations and ration cards, in Vietnam, so we didn't drink too much (right!). So, in order to buy the beer, we had to collect everyone's cards. The beer ration cards bought some forty cases of beer.

The party lasted throughout the night and luck was with us, because there was little to no combat action during our party. At least none that bothered us. We were all drunk and happy. We barbequed steaks and ate fresh vegetables, strawberries and drank beer until we were ready to bust. What a great party for Vietnam. It was the next best thing to sex.

A few days later the new Battery Commander was also getting the party bug. He decided after lunch one day that everyone would have the afternoon off. Then he made sure that several kegs of beer were on hand for a gathering in the mess tent.

The Commander was none other than Philip Sheridan. As I said before, he came from Massachusetts, graduating from an ROTC program at one of the local colleges. He was Executive Officer for a while before being made Commander. He wasn't much older than us, merely a kid and our little group treated him like one. Being new to the job, he decided to do something for the men. We thought it was great. However, the units that needed our combat support thought it sucked. All of the artillery units that normally received our support were on their own for that afternoon. For us, the war could have come to a halt. Most of the aircraft were grounded with minor problems anyway and nothing was going to get repaired because we were all drinking.

There was only one aircraft on the flight line that was still operational, at least according to the paperwork. It was scheduled to take a Colonel on a mission at 15:00 hours. That day I was much thirstier than most. I couldn't wait to get at that beer. After an hour I realized that I was having a hard time walking. Between all the beer and no food, it didn't take long for me to be out of it. I decided to fill my cup one last time and be on my way.

Funny thing happened on the way back to my tent. I came across a jeep, and decided it would be easier to drive back, because I was too drunk to walk. I was having a great time with that jeep until I drove it into a helicopter. But, it was not just any helicopter. No, it was the only helicopter that wasn't grounded. I put a hole in the tail and just missed the tail rotor. The hole I made put the aircraft into a grounded mode. The Colonel was bullshit, to say the least. The only thing I could remember him saying was something about a court martial and spending the rest of the war in a stockade.

A short time later one of the mechanics made a quick repair of the hole allowing the aircraft to fly again. Their mission was an hour late. If the Army didn't give us the time off, and the beer to drink, my ass would have been in a sling.

CHAPTER 20

In 1968, we thought the war was winding down and would soon be over. Several of the men were talking about extending their tours, but most couldn't wait to go home or back to the "world," as we called it. I sometimes think about the men that served in other wars like the men from the Second World War who had to fight for the duration of the war. Knowing that there will always be another battle until it was completely over. Fighting the Germans had to be a bitch of a time. They were hard trained and had unlimited resources. It's no wonder that the war took many lives. But, when the war was finally over, the whole country came out to thank them. Unlike us, returning from Vietnam, we were treated like the scum of the earth.

The WWII veterans were given so many opportunities to expand their horizons, start businesses, money for school or special deals to allow them to purchase homes. Parades were given in their honor throughout the country. It certainly was a wonderful life for most of them.

I can remember when some of the tours were coming to an end, some of the men were rotated back to the States for reassignment and some were preparing themselves to leave the military altogether. The Army had a way of keeping many of the fighting men in Vietnam. They offered them big bonuses. Many men trained in aviation, either pilots or mechanics, were offered at least $10,000 in bonus to stay in and remain at their present location.

The military needed aviation-trained personnel. To some the money looked great. To others, like myself, there wasn't enough money in the world to keep me in that God forsaken country. I hated being in Vietnam, but I did what I agreed to do. 1 didn't run to Canada or to any other place, so I could smoke my dope and let others serve for me. I did what I felt was the proper thing to do.

When I was discharged, I returned to Fort Dix, New Jersey. That was where my military career started. However, this time I was treated with respect by all of the soldiers on base. I remember walking passed a couple of men still in basic training. I thought that their eyes were going to pop out of their heads when they saw my ribbons and combat patch. Of course, it made me feel real proud, and I confess I was a little bit of a show off.

However, my pride was short lived when I hailed an on base cab to go to the bus terminal. The cab driver asked me if I was going to the airport, if so he could drive me there for $75.00.

I said, "You're one hell of a sport. You see a returning Vietnam Vet, you figure I wouldn't care if you screwed me a little more, as long as I made it to the airport a little faster. You want to drive me to the airport for $75.00, when it only costs $10.00 by bus. You're one hell of a guy. If I didn't have to spend more time on base, I would see to it that you weren't allowed back on base, you asshole!"

I left the cab without paying him. I didn't care, I was pissed.

When I arrived in Boston, I couldn't help but smile. I looked through the window of the plane and thought, the nightmare is finally over. I knew that my family was waiting for me inside the terminal ready to take me home. But was the nightmare really over? I knew I was safe now, but the nightly dreams reliving the horrors, the occasional flashbacks that could happen at any time, and the treatment I received for being a Vietnam combat veteran have been both depressing and demoralizing.

Later that day when I was back home in my old room, I slowly removed my uniform. I thought, this is it, my military career is over. I was so different than the boy who left looking for an adventure, and now home felt good.

Many years have passed since Vietnam. I married "my favorite girl" when I returned, and she has been my partner through the tragedies and celebrations that have made up our life. It seems we have always been together. I couldn't imagine life without her.

We have a daughter, who has grown into a beautiful woman. When she was just a baby I could tell that she would do things with her life that I could only dream of doing. Now that she has grown, she has proven me correct. She is not only beautiful, but well-educated and well-traveled living a life I couldn't have even imagined for myself at her age. She has made me very proud of her.

Vietnam, in some ways, made me a hard person. I am so appreciative that both my wife and daughter understood and gave me the love I needed during the bad years. Jobs, like everything else came and went, but they have always been there for me.

Vietnam helped me learn that human connections are important. We have become such a disposable society and it permeates even personal relationships. I have always felt that it is necessary to honor relationships that have supported me in my life.

When you live through an experience like Vietnam, you survive it as part of a team. My entire military experience, especially Vietnam, was a life altering time for me, and I'm sure for everyone who served. The friendships formed there created strong bonds.

When I returned, life happened and so many years went by without reconnecting with the only people in my life who could fully understand that experiences, and its impact on our lives. In the early 90's I was upset with myself for having let so much time lapse without reaching out to these friends. I decided to find them. So, I spent 2 years writing hundreds of letters, making hundreds of telephone calls and traveling thousands of miles, to find those friends. When enough of the men were found, I decided to try and get them together back at Fort Campbell. The "Week of the Eagles" seemed like the perfect time to catch up on our lives...to retell the stories of the times when we were young and wild.

EPILOG

The voice coming over the intercom in the aircraft had a southern drawl to it.

"Ladies and gentleman we are starting our descent into the Nashville Airport, please place your seatbacks in an upright position, and place your tray tables in a locked position for landing."

After 35 years, it was impossible to find all of the guys assigned to our unit during our deployment and service in Vietnam. I was a little disappointed that I couldn't locate more men.

The weather outside of the aircraft was a light rain with high humidity, Of course I wouldn't have expected it to be any other way. As I walked down the ramp to the terminal I could smell that sweet aroma, a mixture of southern rain and grass. The airport had somewhat changed since the last time I was there. It was much larger now, and it seemed to have more passengers bustling through. I had a couple of hours before some of the other men would arrive. We were to meet at the airport information counter, and then travel to the Base together.

The first person I met, and it was really by accident, was Bob Evers. He was lounging, reading a book. We talked about his life in general. He had retired from the New York Police Department after 20 years. He loved the job, but was not making enough money to support his family the way he wanted to. Bob had eight children, and decided to take the retirement and work for a private company for the added income.

After returning to the States in 1968, he had remaining time on his enlistment. He didn't want to sit out 7 or 8 months doing nothing at some nowhere stateside fort, so he requested to return to Vietnam to finish the remainder of his enlistment. He received several more awards for operations against hostile forces.

He played football for the New York Jets minor league for a while, then settled into his life of Police work.

Now jarring the scales at about 300 lbs, his first words were "Russo, you bastard, you're still thin!" Of course, compared to him I'm thin, but I had added a few pounds on here and there myself.

When we turned our discussion to our friends, we remembered when Bill Bader, who had been killed in action, had entered the military. I was told me that he and Bill had long discussions about Bill's home life. Bill told him about his abusive stepfather. He treated Bill, his younger brother and sister badly. Bill entered the service, in part, to escape that situation. He looked forward to the day when he would return and remove his siblings from that situation, but he never did come back. A very sad story.

As Pete came off the ramp from his flight, he had a rather stylish, well-bred looking woman on his arm. As we reconnected, he gave me a hug.

"Russo, you son of a bitch. How the hell are you?" He leaned in toward me whispering in my ear, *"This is not my wife, just a* friend."

I said, "Pete, you bastard, you haven't changed a bit."

He introduced me to his friend, and told me that she was just going to stay a day, then return to California and did I mind.

I said, "Of course not, just what I said, you haven't changed a bit."

They had met in a business meeting and seemed to be attracted immediately. She had been a long time wife of an ex-Marine Major who had retired after doing 20 years in the Corp. His claim to fame according to her, was being stationed in Hawaii for several years. After 15 years of marriage she realized that he was just a big jerk and gave him his walking papers.

For as long as I could remember, Pete always did well with the ladies. Later when we were alone, he explained that he and his wife weren't doing so well together. His friend had offered to share a few nights with him and he accepted.

In 1966, his hometown girlfriend, Joanne followed him to Ft. Campbell from the West Coast. There they lived together, drank together and later she became pregnant, but didn't tell Pete until after he was in Vietnam. Pete only had 8 months left with the military. This gave him an opportunity to be home when she had the baby. After having the baby, they decided that the best thing for all was to give the baby up for adoption, considering they weren't planning on getting married. The baby was adopted. A couple of years later they found themselves back together, and decided to get married. They had a second child that was a boy. Now, they figured it was the time to go and try and regain custody of their first child, a girl. The adoption agency told them that the baby had died. They were stricken with grief for a while. As the years went on they divorced, and went their separate ways. Pete remarried and had a few more children.

In 1999, towards the end of the year, he received a phone call from a woman looking for Joanne, his first wife. Upon inquiring about the reason she wanted to find Joann, He found out that this woman was 30 years old, and was placed for adoption as an infant. He quickly realized that this was his daughter. The same girl that had died, according to the adoption agency.

This was a story you'd read in a novel. He packed a bag, flew to her residence, and then connected with Joanne. They all spent a week together. They explained to her why they had put her up for adoption and how they had tried to find her after they had married. She was very understanding, and it turns out she had enjoyed a wonderful life. She had graduated from college, and was the US Woman's Calf Roping Champion. She also participated in the US Olympics. Pete thought she probably did better with the family that adopted her than she would have with them. It was quite a story.

The next person we bumped into was Zok, Harris Dubin. He didn't see me, but I saw him through a window on the other side of the concourse. He hadn't changed, he was still thin. With the exception of a beard, he was the same old Zok.

Actually, Zok and I had an opportunity to meet a few years before in Atlantic City. He was visiting his mother who lived in Atlantic City. He had his wife and three children with him. They were all so young. There were two boys, one 15 and another 11 and a little girl of 7 yrs. His wife was remarkably young looking and beautiful. They seemed to fit well together. The kids were great. We had a great two days together.

We had continued to send E-Mail messages back and forth throughout most of the later years. His views are a little different than mine when it comes to the establishment or maybe just the military. Of course many of his views would be from the 60's. He had no trust in the government or the military, and didn't want anything to do with the system. Unfortunately, there are many Vietnam Veterans that feel the same. They mistrust a system that did virtually nothing for the Vets after returning home.

We met Fred Brown, Claude Boone and Phil Sheridan at the motel. In the meantime, we had some drinks at the bar while waiting for a person that wasn't mentioned. His name is Ray Brerenton. Ray was one of the last minute replacements prior to departing Vietnam. He lived in New Jersey, and has his own business.

We finally got the whole group together, and it was wild. Trying to place all the bags and all of the people into the little rental Van was like trying to fit everyone into a sports car. The whole ordeal reminded me of the time back in Vietnam when we decided to sneak down to Cameron Bay for a couple of nights. Cameron Bay was a peninsula off of the coast of Vietnam. We couldn't understand why the men stationed there were receiving Combat Duty pay. It was like being in the States. Lights on all night, bars, movies, it was unbelievable.

We met at a predetermined location outside of Div-Arty's landing pad at Camp Eagle, and loaded the men and their bags.

"Hey Russo, you got any room up there for this bag? Maybe you can sit on it while you're flying?"

"Are you out of your fuck'n mind, just pack it down as hard as you can, then you sit on it?"

"Where is the beer? I see it, no wonder you can't fit anything back there, and you guys have too much ice in that poncho cover."

"Hey, I need to keep the beer cold, don't you know?"

"Fuck'n A, —Alright Pete, pass me one before you sit on it."

"Hey Zok, see if you can fit this stuff over on your side."

"Fuck off move, I don't have any room over here."

It was like a bunch of guys heading for spring break back home, instead of making a night flight in Vietnam. The beer was cold, the weather was hot, and I was, what we would call, shit-faced, before we were half way there. I was lucky to find the way at all. It was extra dark by the time we arrived and the instruments were awfully blurry. We did get there, and we somehow managed to land without incident, to our surprise.

Now, it was over 30 years later, the guys were older and only 'somewhat matured. Now at Fort Campbell, we talked about the things we did in and around the Base. Fred Brown who had retired a Sgt. Major had his grandson Jake with him. Jake was about 7 years old, and anyone could tell that he loved his grandfather. Fred told us about an easy way to get back into the base airfield to watch the ceremonies of the "Week of the Eagles" without getting trapped in the traffic. We slipped in and around several streets until a roadblock of MP's stopped me.

"Sir, can I see your On-Post Pass please?"

"Well" I said, "I'm just going to pahk so we can watch the ceremony."

"What did you say, Sir?"

"I said pahk"

"Say that again Sir?"

"I said, pahk. You know pahk."

At that point, everyone in the van burst out laughing.

"Hey Russo, he doesn't understand that Boston accent."

"The MP just told us to park wherever you want to."

We parked in an area on the far side of the airfield. It was hot, really hot. The temperature was going into the 90's, and we were out in the middle of an airfield with no cover. They did have ice cold water. Portable truck containers full. Good decision. That day was called Super Saturday. It was part of the Week of the Eagles Ceremonies. The ceremonies started with the welcome to all of the returning Screaming Eagles. We had past 101" members from the 2nd World War. Some of these men jumped into battle on D-day and had just returned from making the same jump at 80 years old. 101" was at Vietnam, Desert Storm and a host of other conflicts. The 101" Skydiving Team did a show, and there were demonstrations of the history of aircraft and combat techniques from both WW2 and Vietnam to the current advancements. We saw two helicopters refuel in the air at the same time, and a demonstration of an airlift command aircraft land, backup, and take back off with little to no runway, amazing!

"Jake buddy, I need more water, how about it pal?"

I was pouring the water over my head to keep from cooking. I didn't bring a hat, like most of the guys. We made Jake the designated water boy. The Super Saturday proceedings took all day Saturday. They had food vendors for lunch. The typical hot dogs and hamburgers. I even saw Zok eat a hamburger, and he's a vegetarian. We were starved, hot and thirsty, but all in all, it was a great day.

Returning to the motel we decided to stop at a military store. There were many military items to choose from. We picked up pins and miniature medals and a bunch of items we should have bought when leaving the service.

It was in this store that I told the guys about receiving the Air Medal and Bronze Star a couple of years ago.

"Can you guys believe this? After 25 years, I finally received my Bronze Star and Air Medal. I received two clusters for my Air Medal, but never the medal and I wanted it. I petitioned the Army several times, with no luck. So I tried my local Senator's office. He was supposed to be this big man when it came to Veterans. I would send him a letter. His office would ask for more information, I sent it to him. A year would go by, I heard nothing from his office. I had the Battery Commander and several of the guys sign a letter stating I was to be awarded the medal, but never received it. Finally, just after a Senate election, I wrote to the Senator and said the following; 'it doesn't look good for a Senator when he can't get something done for a Veteran. When the Veteran has waited 25 to 30 years for something he deserved. Still, I had to prove my case with very little help from him. I finally received the Air Medal and Bronze Star. I found the medals in an insulated envelope on the floor of my front porch. It was just lying there. How great does one feel when something like that happens? Still to this day I'm owed the Army Commendation Medal. I am not going to hold my breath for it. I have written off that Senator."

In the store they had every military insignia, uniform or piece of equipment imaginable. They even had small military toys, replicas for the kids. We did some shopping and returned back to the motel.

As we were pulling up to the motel, Phil Sheridan said, "Hey look guys, I have some 8mm films taken back at Camp Eagle, and my R & R at Sidney, Australia. Come over to my room in few minutes and take a look at them."

It was a great idea. He even carried an old projector with him all the way from Massachusetts. The movies were really good. Some of the guys, including me, brought some still shots taken of us back then. Some were taken in Vietnam, some were from Ft. Campbell and some were from Nashville. Sheridan had drinks, snacks and provided a comfortable place to enjoy it all. We had a great time.

Before returning to our rooms, we talked about the girls we had back then. I asked Zok if he ever saw the baby his girl had. He told me that she was never pregnant.

"But she stopped writing to me when I asked for a picture of her naked. She told me to fuck off, I never heard from her again."

Well Zok, here's your chance, why don't you give her a call."

"Maybe I'll look her name up in the phone book and see if it's in there. How about you' Russo? Where was that girl that you were screwing? Wasn't she a student nurse?"

"Yes she was, she came from a town south of Nashville called Lebanon, I think. I asked the clerk at the desk for a phone book that covered that town. He said, that they didn't have one here. The town was about an hour south of Nashville. Besides, even if she kept her maiden name all of these years, what good would it do me to call her. She's probably still pissed at me from the 60's. I think I messed her mind up pretty good.

Her father was a retired Navy man. I went there one year for Thanksgiving Dinner, and my car broke down. He had to come and get me on the highway. He was a farmer. I don't think he liked me too much. Anyway, I don't think I want to talk to her now after all these years. However, there is one that I wouldn't mind trying to find. She was a girl who lived in Virginia when I was in school. She had long blond hair, and a body to die for. Or, maybe I'll just forget about it. Those days are long gone."

Around that time, Bob spoke up and said, "look, we're now in our 50's, I think it would be a great idea if we all got tattoos of the 101st patch on our arms, what do you think?"

I said, "If you get tattoos it should be on the combat side. Usually, the 101" insignia is placed on ones left arm, indicating ones present assignment. If the patch is placed on the right arm, it means that the person served in combat with that Division."

"Of course" said Pete, "That's a great idea. Let's do it, and let's get jump wings on our chest. What do you think? Let's all do it."

Zok, "I can't do it. I just told my son that he couldn't get a tattoo. How is it going to look if I come home with one? No way."

Bob, "Look we're all older now, there's no reason why we can't do what we want. I want to get one, my daughter dared me. She would never believe that I would actually go and get one. Let's go tonight."

Pete, "You guys don't have a hair on your ass if you don't do this."

That evening, we went into Clarksville.

Pete, "The motel manager gave me directions to the best tattoo parlor in Clarksville. I'll give you directions."

It was dark when we eventually found the Tattoo Parlor. It was located in the middle of the old part of town that was currently being renovated. Across the street was a very large nightclub. They were opening the large windows that led out to the street.

Pete, "OK let's go."

Brerenton said, "Not me, I'm not going to get one. I went all of my life without one, I am not going to get one now."

We all went into the shop. There were pictures of tattoos everywhere. As we strolled in, there was a girl having her belly button pierced. Someone said, I guess this place does it all.

Pete and Bob told the owner what they wanted. The owner skimmed through his books until he found the Screaming Eagle Patch.

Zok, "I don't think I'm going to get a full patch. Maybe I'll just get Airborne, on my arm and jump wings on my chest. I can't believe I am going to do this, my wife is going to get really pissed at me, not to mention hearing from my son."

The owner wrote the contracts for each of them, and they paid the asking price.

"Russo, aren't you getting a tattoo?"

"Oh sure I am," I said not trying to hide my sarcasm, "I told my daughter, the Law School Graduate that she better not get one if she knows what's good for her."

Zok, "I think she's a little old for you to be telling her what she can or can't do."

I said, "As long as she's my daughter, she better listen."

As Bob was placed into a chair, the tattoo artist was collecting his tools. The owner, had just placed a girl into a second chair to start on her. She took off her top and exposed her breast. She was about 24, and had great looking breasts. We just watched. Poor Bob couldn't see because he was in a chair facing the opposite side of the room. We, on the other hand, had first class seats. The owner took her right breast in his hand, and started to draw a design on it. She then got up and nonchalantly walked over to the mirror to check it out. She liked it, so they started. I went out to the van, and decided to call home.

"Hi Hon, what's going on at home?"

Nothing was different and everything was fine. My wife asked where I was, and what was I doing. I told her.

"I'm at a tattoo parlor with the guys. They're going to have the combat patches tattooed on."

"You know, you'll never hear the end of it with your daughter if you get one. You told her that she couldn't have one. How is it going to look if you come home with one?"

I said, "Hon, I'm not going to get one, forget about it, I'm not."

I told her what we had been up to and how much fun we were having together.

"It's like we were never apart, not one of us turned out bad."

It was true, we all made a fair living, and we all thought that our military experience made us better civilians.

After the phone call I went across the street and had a beer with Brerenton and Sheridan.

Brerenton, "See that girl sitting in the corner? She's a Captain, and owns that Harley parked outside. She's a pretty good-looking babe, if you ask me.

I said, "I think I'll go over and say hello."

"Do you mind if I sit with you? I understand that you're a captain in the 101", is that true?"

She said, "Yes I am. Are with the old guys that fought in Vietnam?"

I felt a little degraded. What does she mean 'old guys?

I said, "Yes, I am with the older men. But you know, we aren't really that old."

She laughed, "Oh I didn't mean it that way. Actually, you guys don't look too bad, considering what I have to choose from these days."

"Well", I said, "when the guys are done across the street, we'll come over and buy you a beer and tell you some real war stories."

"Thanks", she said, "But I'm heading back to Camp. If you remember, 04:30 hours is very early."

I finished my beer, and returned to the tattoo parlor.

Zok, was sitting at the counter talking to the owner.

"I don't think I'm going to have this tattoo done after all. I've changed my mind."

The owner said, "Well, you signed the agreement and the agreement states that there is no refund if you change your mind."

I jumped in, "I'd like to see that agreement."

So the owner took out a blank agreement form to show me.

I then asked the owner, "Where's the one he signed?"

I was going to rip it up if he passed it to me. He probably knew what was on my mind. When the owner went into the other room, I said to Zok, "Fuck him. If you want your money back, we'll get it back."

As the owner returned to the room, I said, loud enough for him to hear, "How much do you think this electronic cash register will cost if I throw it through the window?" I thought to myself, it would be kind of cool if I return home sporting a black eye.

The owner made like he didn't hear me, and just walked back into the other room.

Zok said, "Russo don't worry, if I wanted my money back that bad I would do what I have to do to get it. I guess, I'll just go ahead and do it. Besides, I'm going to tell my wife that it was all your fault that we got these tattoos."

As the girl finished receiving her boob tattoo, she walked over to the mirror to check it out. She was about breast height to Bob's face as he sat in the chair. She turned to him, stuck her boob into his face and said, "What do you think do you like it?"

We couldn't see Bob's face, but we could tell that he was laughing from the way his back was jiggling.

The next day we were scheduled to eat lunch and dinner at the Vietnam Veterans Association. We went to their hospitality suite, and decided to have a few drinks. As Pete and Zok received their drinks, the bartender turned to them.

"Hey, how about a tip for the bartender?"

The bar tender was a retired First Sergeant, and had the attitude of asshole. It was just this type of person that stopped me from joining other Veteran's organizations. His attitude was pissing me off. I asked for a beer, he gave it to me and said, "I expect a buck."

I looked at him and said, "Keep expecting." I walked outside. It was a very hot and humid day. Two wonderful looking older ladies went into the room. They were very poised and well dressed. They started a conversation with the bartender. I went in to listen. One of the women was telling him that they were there representing a Retired General and Colonel. The bartender asked her for their names. I couldn't hear the first name, but I did hear the Colonial's name. It was Colonial Tallon. The bartender said, "Who the hell are they? I never heard of them (he was a real nasty person).

The other woman said, "You've never heard of them, and you were in the 101st"? Well, at least give us a couple of cool drinks before we leave. As the women were leaving, I went to them and apologized.

"Ladies, let me apologize for that rude ignorant person. I do know Colonial Tallon, his wife and his daughter Mary."

She said, "That's Mary Elizabeth. She's a very lovely person."

I said, "I'm sure she is. Please send my regards to the Colonial and his family. Tell them I have fond memories of them at Fort Campbell. Ladies, please don't judge us all by the way that arrogant person treated you."

She answered, "Not at all."

Later that evening we were trying to decide what we were going to do for dinner. Should we go to the Vietnam Vets Banquet or not?

I said, "I don't care if we did pay for dinner. Fuck them. They can keep the money."

Zok, "I don't want to go either. Fuck them."

Phil said, "Look, I paid for that dinner, I want to at least get a couple of drinks for my money."

So, we agreed that we would go there, eat then leave.

When we arrived at the dinner, most of the people were sitting at their tables. The association officers were giving speeches and awards. The arrogant bastard that gave the woman a hard time was receiving an award for all of his contributions.

I said, "That asshole! I think I'm going to be sick."

Bob said, "OK guys, let's not have any trouble tonight. OK guys. No trouble guys."

Nevertheless, he did receive an award. As he received the award, he broke down and cried. Immediately leaving the room. I was amazed.

Early next morning, I went to Pete's room, to see if he was up. It was approaching the time to start packing for home. Pete came to the door completely nude.

He said, "Oh, I thought it may be the maid for my early morning massage."

Everyone piled into Bob's room. We talked about our jump training, Fort Campbell, the bars at Fort Campbell. The women that were in our lives back then. Vietnam, after Vietnam. We laughed, drank some beer and talked some more. I think all of us said a quiet prayer for the men that we left behind, like Lt. Mullins. In 1994 I was contacted by an organization in Washington, DC. The organization is a non-profit company that, by request, works to locate friends and family members of those who had died in Vietnam. Lt. Mullin's daughter contacted me. She was the baby born after her father's death. We still exchange letters or greetings around the holidays. Some of the best men never made it to the reunion because they never came back.

We all agreed that we would try and meet at least once per year. At the airport, the guys walked me to my ramp to see me off. I turned to Zok, as they called my flight to board and stuck out my hand to shake and say goodbye. He slapped my hand, and gave me a hug. The rest of the guys followed suit. It was a very moving. As I turned back for the final time, Pete yelled, "Let's meet again next year. Don't forget!"

Most of us made the trip to bring closure to that time of our life, but once we were together it was the good times we remembered most. This was a wonderful trip allowing us to catch up on our lives and to take a glimpse back...back to a time **when minutes seemed like hours.**

www.ingramcontent.com/pod-product-compliance
Lightning Source LLC
LaVergne TN
LVHW081552060526
838201LV00054B/1866